Wassim El Kadhi

Cross-Cultural Destination Image Assessment:

Cultural segmentation versus the global tourist

An Exploratory study of Arab-Islamic and Protestant European youths' pre-visitation image on Berlin.

Diplomica® Verlag GmbH

El Kadhi, Wassim: Cross-Cultural Destination Image Assessment: Cultural segmentation versus the global tourist. An Exploratory study of Arab-Islamic and Protestant European youths' pre-visitation image on Berlin, Hamburg, Diplomica Verlag GmbH 2009

ISBN: 978-3-8366-7223-8
Druck Diplomica® Verlag GmbH, Hamburg, 2009

Bibliografische Information der Deutschen Bibliothek
Die Deutsche Bibliothek verzeichnet diese Publikation in der Deutschen Nationalbibliografie;
detaillierte bibliografische Daten sind im Internet über
<http://dnb.ddb.de> abrufbar.

© Diplomica Verlag GmbH
http://www.diplomica.de, Hamburg 2009
Printed in Germany

Abstract

Destination image is considered as the key in attracting tourists. This study purported to scrutinise whether Berlin's tourist authorities have to consider cultural segmentation when developing marketing strategies relating to the place's image. As an exploratory study, it examined Berlin's image among youths from Arab-Islamic and Protestant European countries and confronted them. In an era that is subjected to globalisation and refers to the global tourist, it is vindicated to pose this question. Various scholars are convinced that the world tourism market may be treated as a homogenous one due to globalisation. However, the literature also provides some opposing bearings and discusses them. It further gives some background information on Berlin as a tourist destination, addresses destination image concerning influential cultural factors and the implications of globalisation on consumer behaviour. Finally, it studies the Arab-Islamic and Protestant European youth cultures in the light of globalisation and possible modifying effects.

In response to the objectives of this study, primary research was conducted. It involved both quantitative and qualitative data collection methods. Field and online surveys enabled the researcher to collect 239 completed questionnaires (103 Arab-Islamic and 136 Protestant European youths). Besides semi-structured interviews and focus group discussions were carried out at EF Language School, Bournemouth. Following the completion of the survey, obtained data was entered into SPSS. Frequencies and means were calculated for each variable and several ANOVA tests and cross-tabulations conducted in order to stress destination image's specificity in terms of cultural background.

Research findings revealed significant differences between the groups regarding their perception of Berlin. Arab-Islamic youths had a more negative stance towards Berlin than their counterparts. Not only did divergences occur between the groups, but also within the groups. Thus, destination image is culture-specific and may also vary across countries sharing similar cultural backgrounds. Overall, despite the effects of globalisation, cultural market segmentation still remains a vital element for a tourist place such as Berlin where the image management is concerned. The research project provides recommendations for Berlin congruent with the outcomes and concludes with the provision of recommendations for further research.

Acknowledgements

At this point I would like to take the opportunity to thank all those people that have supported me during the completion of my project.

First of all, I would like to express my deepest gratitude and appreciation to my parents and my grandmother who have made the last study year possible thanks to their financial contribution. In particular, very special thanks to my grandmother who is very ill and has unfortunately been to hospital since the beginning of July. I dedicate this work to her.

Secondly, a big thanks to my girl-friend Verena, whose support and kind words of encouragement in bad times enabled me to remain optimistic. Thank you very much.

Also, I would like to thank Reinhold and Sylvia Reis, the parents of my girl-friend Verena, who supported us whenever they had the opportunity to do so. Thanks a lot.

I would like to extend heartfelt thanks to my supervisor Ton van Egmond, for his helpful guidance right the way through the writing of this book. Also here a special thanks to him.

Finally, I am additionally grateful to all the people that supported me in conducting primary research. Thanks to all survey participants, interviewees and to EF School, Bournemouth and especially to my Jordanian friend Houssam who was so kind to support me in arranging as many Arab-Islamic surveyees as possible.

Word Count: 21, 739

Table of Contents

List of Tables

List of Figures

List of Appendices

List of Abbreviations

ANOVA	Analysis of Variance
BPB	German Federal Centre for Political Education
BTM	Berlin Tourism Marketing GmbH
C&W/H&B	Property consultant Cushman & Wakefield Healey & Baker
F	Female
FAZ	Frankfurter Allgemeine Zeitung
GAWC	Globalisation and World Cities Group
M	Male
UAE	United Arab Emirates
UK	United Kingdom
USA	United States of America
WVS	World Values Survey Association

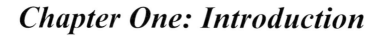

Chapter One: Introduction

1.1   Introduction

The travel and tourism industry is one of the world's largest employers, creating over 231 million jobs worldwide (WTTC 2008) and growing steadily at disproportionally high rates compared to other industries as a result of globally spreading wealth, which makes tourism more international (UNWTO 2008a).

The growing internationality in tourism is part of an on-going globalisation process. Possible implications of globalisation are the homogenisation of cultures, which may induce more homogenous preferences and tastes across diverse societies (Buttaro 2005, CATO Institute 2003). Cultural diversity is being lost to homogeneity nearly everywhere in the world (Redford & Brosius 2006). In this context, Barber (cited CATO Institute 2003:9) cites an interesting statement of a Bayer AG Manager: '*A lie has been perpetuated for years and years. The lie is that people are different!*'

Back in the 1980's, Plog (1990 cited Kozak *et al.* 2003) mentioned that a tourist should not be examined by his cultural background. He referred to the global tourist, which means that the world tourism market may be treated as a homogenous market. Since the 1980's, the world has extensively developed, especially technologically, and is evermore merging (Nuscheler 2006, Stahel *et al.* 2008). Isizoh (2006, p.155) talks of the 'global village' and of the shrinking world, which is progressively merging in terms of culture, religion and language due to technological developments, such as the Internet and fast travel. The latter factors mean that people around the globe are more easily subjected to the same lifestyles and to growing globalisation of cultures. In particular, the dominant Western culture is increasingly absorbed by marginal cultures, which are in jeopardy of losing cultural integrity (Chang *et al.* 2006).

So what could this all mean for the tourism industry or, in the case of this study, for Berlin as a tourist destination? A destination such as Berlin attracts tourists from around the world and from various cultural backgrounds. In order to attract tourists from diverse cultural backgrounds, the city of Berlin develops marketing strategies that are tailor-made for each of its source markets and respond to cultural preferences (Gruber 2008). However, is cultural segmentation necessary in an era where globalisation apparently induces homogenisation in people's preferences and tastes across cultures? If it is not, a tourist destination, such as Berlin could reduce its marketing expenditure, as it would be able to adopt identical strategies across cultures. Therefore, this exploratory study scrutinises a vital part of marketing, namely destination image, and intends to identify whether Arab-Islamic and Protestant European youths (see 1.4.1) homogenously perceive Berlin as a tourist destination. Youths are especially prone to globalisation and gradually adopt the 'Coca Cola' culture (Pelkington *et al.* 2002, Zahid 2007), as they are more proficient with the Internet and hence experience dimensions that former generations never knew. The youth market is the market of the future; consequently, it is vital for the tourism industry to understand it.

Among young tourists, Berlin is a fashionable tourism destination due to a variety of cultural and entertainment based offers. In recent years, Berlin has generally become a very successful tourist destination and the most visited German city, not only among Germans, but also among international tourists. About 38% of 17.3 million overnight stays were made by foreigners in 2007, an increase of approximately 17% on 2006 (BTM 2007). Most came from the UK, the Netherlands, Italy, Spain and Denmark, with only a minor number from the Arab world. Previous image studies have shown that Berlin is quite popular among tourists due to its interesting history, the variety of cultural activities, its rich gastronomy offer, and its multi-cultural society and favourable price level (Habermann *et al* 2006). Hence, Berlin's image among tourists is generally known; however, the author could not locate any sources that show how the city's image may vary from place to place, which again justifies this study.

Destination image is a crucial part of destination management and considered as the key in attracting tourists (Cooper *et al.* 2005, Echtner & Brent Ritchie 2003, Frochot & Legohére 2007, p. 176, Kim & Richardson 2003, Kozak *et al.* 2004). Due to the growing internationality of the tourism market, identifying the perceived image of tourists from various cultural backgrounds is becoming more complicated; however, it also becomes more important. Regarding destination image alone, a very limited number of studies have been carried out, not to speak of the studies from a cross-cultural point of view. The topic of how tourists from different cultural backgrounds are at variance in their perceived destination image is basically under-researched (*Kozak et* al. 2004). Besides, the studies that investigate destination image in cultural terms are contradictory. The majority of sources claim that cultural factors influence the image formation process (Pizam cited Kozak *et al.* 2003), while others maintain the contrary (Plog cited Kozak *et al.* 2003). Plog (cited Kozak *et al.* 2003) proposes that the rapid globalisation of the tourist phenomenon brings about an enhanced understanding of the *'global tourist'*. The on-going globalisation process, which is potentially modifying the way that people live and behave supports Plog's assumption. International tourism can be considered as part of the globalisation process (Macleod 2004, p.8; Reid 2003, p.13), which may induce changing behavioural patterns within cultures and their people.

To conclude, it is this study's aim to identify whether there is a correlation between cultural background and the perception of Berlin between Arab-Islamic and Protestant European youth. The question arises, as a consequence of the on-going globalisation process, which is considered by many scholars as bringing about cultural homogenisation, as well as homogenous consumer preferences across cultures.

1.2   Rationale

In a period in which the business climate is worsening due to events such as the credit crunch, it may be important for organisations to cut expenditures. In future, the city of Berlin could be able to reduce its marketing expenditures for the management of its image, if it was found that people across cultures do not differ in their perception of a place.

Berlin has been chosen as the case study, since Berlin's tourism authorities have consented to support this study by providing supportive documents. Berlin's image as a tourist destination is generally known, but not how it may differ among people from varying cultural backgrounds. Little is known about Arab tourists in particular, which justifies opting for these tourists to be studied. Due to the author's contacts with people from the Arab and Western worlds, he is able to capture a relatively high number of interviewees from both cultural backgrounds. Consequently, an expressive comparative study is more likely and will enhance the study's validity.

The focal point lies on the youth market, since it composes tomorrow's market and is currently the largest growing segment in tourism (WYSE 2007). The youth market is often under-rated; even though travellers aged 16-24 represent about 20% of all international tourists. What is more, its budget reputation is not vindicated. In fact the average spend per trip has improved by 40% since 2004 to 1,915 Euros in 2007, making youths a fairly noteworthy market for destination managers (Mintel 2006a, UNWTO 2008b).

Cross-cultural research in tourism has received increasing vigilance from scholars in recent years (Kozak *et al.* 2003, Reisinger & Turner 2003, p. xxi), nonetheless, compared with other fields of tourism research, cross-cultural studies are almost entirely missing (van Egmond 2005, p. 8). Especially in destination image, cross-cultural studies are scarce (Kozak *et al.* 2004). The growing internationality of the tourism market makes cross-cultural studies increasingly imperative (Reisinger & Turner 2003, p.29), because prior cross-cultural studies were contradictory with some sources claiming culture-specificity of tourism, while others claim the contrary (see 3.5). The aim of undertaking cross-cultural research is to scrutinise other cultures, to gain knowledge of them and to test cultural differences in tourism marketing contexts (Kozak *et al.* 2004). It is vital for destination management to study the profile of its customers, particularly their behaviour, preferences and values in order to apply efficient positioning and market segmentation strategies (Reisinger & Turner 2002a). Schiffman and Kanuk (1991, p.464) add that an understanding of *'the similarities and differences that exist between nations is critical to the multinational marketer'* and Berlin can be regarded as such.

1.3   Aims and Objectives

Figure 1.1 demonstrates the research framework of this study. The research project aims to find an answer to the following question:

> ***'Do Berlin's tourist authorities have to consider cultural segmentation when developing marketing strategies relating to the place's image in an era that refers to the global tourist?'***

The author has identified six research objectives in order to meet the overall aim of his study. These are:

- To examine previous image studies on Berlin and Germany, as tourist destinations.

- To review the literature and to identify the importance of destination image, as well as the factors, including cultural factors that influence individuals' image of a destination.

- To examine whether the globalisation process is influencing people's behaviour in general and whether globalisation induces a more homogenous lifestyle, especially among youths.

- To examine the Arab-Islamic and the Protestant European culture in general and the relevant youth cultures and to identify differences and similarities.

- To survey a sample of Arab-Islamic and Protestant European youth on their image of Berlin as a tourist destination by distributing online-surveys and conducting semi-structured interviews.

- To identify if there are cross-cultural differences in the perception of Berlin as a tourist destination among Arab-Islamic and Protestant European youth?

Figure 1.1: Research Framework

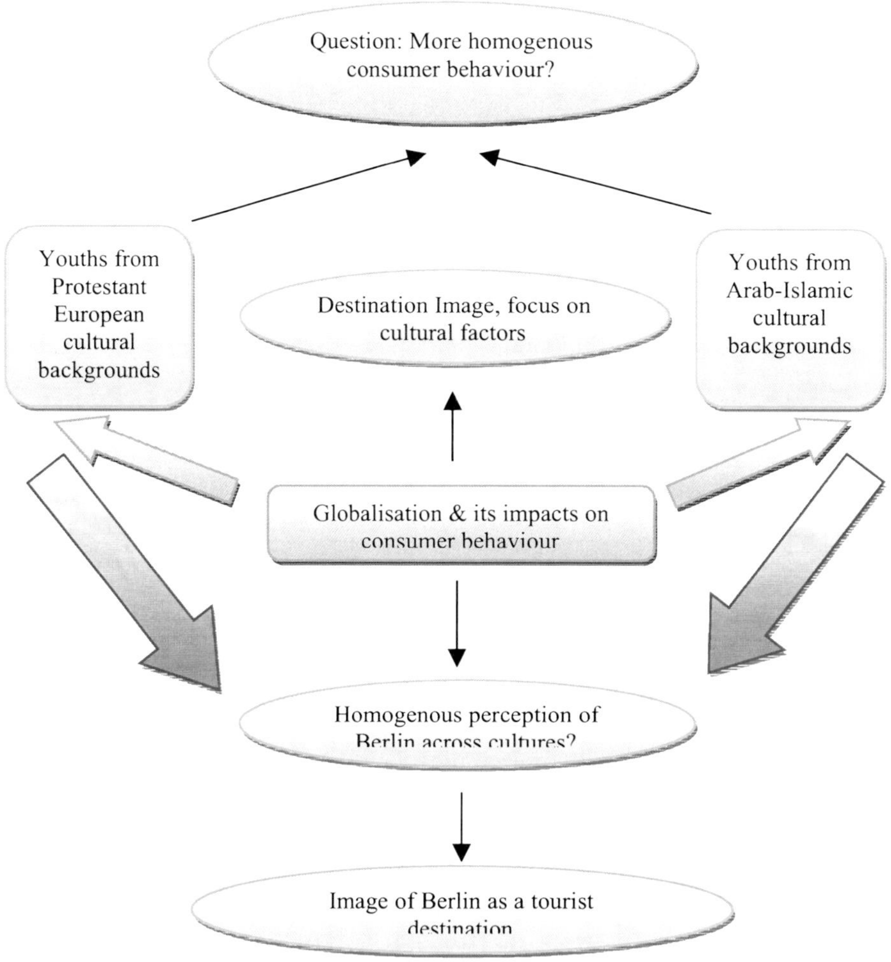

1.4   Definition of terms

1.4.1   Who is meant by "Protestant European"?

The prevailing culture of European origin is often referred to as Western culture. Western culture depicts on Greek notions, Roman law, the Latin language and Christian expectations (Lashbrook 1969, van Egmond 2005). Nowadays, Western culture dominates in Western and Central European nations and in various countries in which European descendents reside, such as the US and Australia. Due to the roots of Western culture, it is assumed that people share similar behavioural patterns; however, Western Europe can be divided into two parts, culture-wise.

Northern/Western Europe is characterised by the Protestant ethic, while Southern/Western Europe is characterised by the Catholic ethic (Doyle 1986, p.151).

Why did the inner European-division take place? In the age of religious wars from the 16th to the 18th century, violence among Roman Catholics and Protestants dominated life across Europe (Pearson Education 2008). At the end of the war, Europe found itself in a period of religious reformation and was divided into different creeds (Doyle 1986, p. 151). The religious division took place in almost every sense, both in terms of varying interpretations of the Christian doctrine and practices and historical traditions. Consequently, Protestant and Catholic Europe emerged that both developed diverging values. Nowadays, a variety of scholars from varying research areas claim the existence of cultural differences between the groups (Kanniainen & Pääkkönen 2007, Randell-Moon 2006, Sullins 1999).

However, Catholicism and Protestantism both include the forms of Christian faith and practice that originated with the principles of the Reformation (Oxford Dictionary 2008). The value systems of the Protestants have influenced a variety of cultures in Europe (van Egmond 2005, p.18). The countries that have been influenced are Denmark, Finland, Germany, Iceland, the Netherlands, Norway, Sweden, Switzerland, Great Britain and Austria. Inglehart (cited Inglehart & Baker 2000) conducted world value surveys from 1990 to 1991 and from 1995 to 1998 examining different regions and ethnicities by their cultural context and illustrating the phenomena with the aid of a cultural value map (Appendix 1). As a result, he deduced that the countries mentioned above share similar values and beliefs, which are partly affected by the economic success of these countries. Although, the UK and Austria are not part of Protestant Europe in his map, it is widely acknowledged that these countries hold Protestant values (Delacroix & Nielsen 2001, van Egmond 2005, p. 18-19). People from Protestant countries are considered to demonstrate common behavioural patterns in terms of *'thinking, feeling and acting'* (Hofstede 1991 cited van Egmond 2005, p. 19) and will thus be regarded as one market for the purpose of this study.

1.4.2   Who is meant by "Arab-Islamic"?

The Arab world comprises 24 countries and stretches from the Arabian Sea in the east to the Atlantic Ocean in the west (Figure 1.2). The majority of people within the Arab world share the same religion, the Islam. It is also the source of Arabic culture and Arabic language and is the reason why the Arab world displays many similarities in terms of lifestyle (Altawajiri 1998).

Figure 1.2: The Arab World

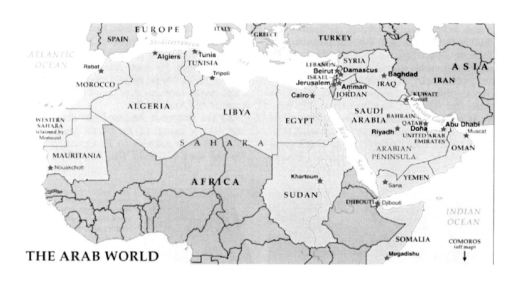

Source: Oneclimate.net 2007

However, not all countries within the Arab world are lucrative from a destination manager's perspective, since only the Arab countries in the Middle East expose notable numbers of outbound tourists. The five countries with the highest profile in terms of outbound tourist expenditure are the UAE, Saudi Arabia, Kuwait, Egypt and Syria (Mintel 2006b). However, the other Middle Eastern countries, such as Yemen, Oman, Qatar, Bahrain and Jordan may also be quite lucrative markets due to their 'oil money' (Mintel 2004). Consequently, all the Middle Eastern and Gulf countries mentioned above will be considered as the Arab world throughout this book. Like traditionally Protestant European, Arab-Islamic from the Middle East also demonstrate common behavioural patterns where thinking, feeling and acting is concerned, and will thus be treated as one group for the purpose of this study.

According to Hofstede (2001, p.52) the Middle East can be regarded as a culturally homogenous region.

1.4.3 The youth market

A universal definition on the youth market does not seem to exist. While the UN defines youth as people between 15 to 24 years (cited UNESCO 2006), the UNWTO (cited Mintel 2006c) adopts an upper age limit of 25 years. However, there is a trend for setting the upper age limit even higher, up to 30 years of age and more due to current social changes (Mintel 2006c).

People are considered as youths as long as they live at their parental home, are full-time students and are financially dependent to a certain degree. Since, the European and the Middle Eastern education systems imply that most students will graduate at the age of 23 to 25; the author has decided to adopt UNWTO's definition which sets the age limit to 25 years and is a major player within the tourism industry.

1.4.4 Culture

Culture is widely defined as *'the set of customs, values, norms, beliefs, habits, arts and patterns of lifestyle shared by a group of people or society'* (Reisinger & Turner 2002b, Khang & Moscardo 2006). It is the spirit of a country and the mark of its identity (Altwaijri 1998). Altwaijri (1998) claims all nations possess their own culture and demonstrate a distinct lifestyle. Thus, culture holds human groups together, since it is considered as the way of life by homogenous groups (Harris & Moran 1979 cited Reisinger & Turner 2002b). Culture is also a guide to behavioural patterns that develop rules of social behaviour and perceptions and lead to similar ways of feeling and thinking about things within a human group of the same cultural background (Khang & Moscardo 2006, Reisinger & Turner 2002b, Truong & King 2006).

Concerning the purpose of this project, it may be helpful to understand that the meaning of culture slightly differs in Arabic, although the definitions above are also part of the term's definition here. In addition though, the word 'culture' is increasingly being used in regard to *'the intellectual, literary and social progress of individuals and communities'* (Altwaijri 1998). According to Altwaijri (1998) it means '*to refine the soul, speech and intelligence'*. Al-Muhit (cited Altwaijri 1998) defines the term culture as follows: '*to become intelligent, agile, and smart; to straighten the lance, to make straight'*. Altogether this demonstrates that the Arab definition rather considers culture in terms of how cultivated groups of humans and their individuals are.

1.5 Chapter overview

This research study is divided into seven chapters. A summary of each chapter is:

1.5.1 Chapter One: Introduction

This chapter introduces the studied topic and vindicates the necessity for scrutinising this research area. Subsequently, the research aim and objectives are presented and certain key terms defined that are utilised throughout the book.

1.5.2 Chapter Two: Berlin as a tourist destination

This chapter provides background information on Berlin and on Germany as tourist destinations. It also presents previous destination image studies on Berlin.

1.5.3 Chapter Three: Literature Review I Destination image

This chapter provides an accurate analysis of destination image. The term is being defined and the factors that impinge on the formation of image examined, including cultural factors.

1.5.4 Chapter Four: Literature Review II Globalisation: Its effects on consumer behaviour. Comparing Arab-Islamic and Protestant European Culture

This chapter investigates the implications of globalisation on consumer behaviour. Afterwards, the Arab-Islamic and Protestant European culture, in particular the respective youth cultures, are examined and compared in order to identify cultural similarities and differences.

1.5.5 Chapter Five: Methodology

This chapter demonstrates the methodological framework of this study. It shows how primary research was conducted and unveils the limitations of this study.

1.5.6 Chapter Six: Data analysis and findings

This chapter presents the most connoting primary findings and analyses them by focalising on identifying correlations between cultural background and the perception of a place.

1.5.7 Chapter Seven: Conclusion and recommendations

Prior to concluding the research project, this chapter discusses the findings of primary research and the literature review. Subsequently, recommendations are made to Berlin's tourist authorities along with suggestions for further research.

1.6 Summary

This chapter has introduced the research project to the reader. The study's aim and objectives were explained, as well as the structure of this work. The next chapter provides background information on Berlin and Germany as tourist destinations.

Chapter Two: Berlin as a tourist destination

2.1 Introduction

This chapter introduces Berlin as a tourist destination with Berlin's attributes being presented, as well as facts and figures concerning its tourism industry. Furthermore, Germany's image will be scrutinised in terms of tourism prior to focussing on previous image studies regarding Berlin. An overview is illustrated in figure 2.1.

Figure 2.1: Chapter overview

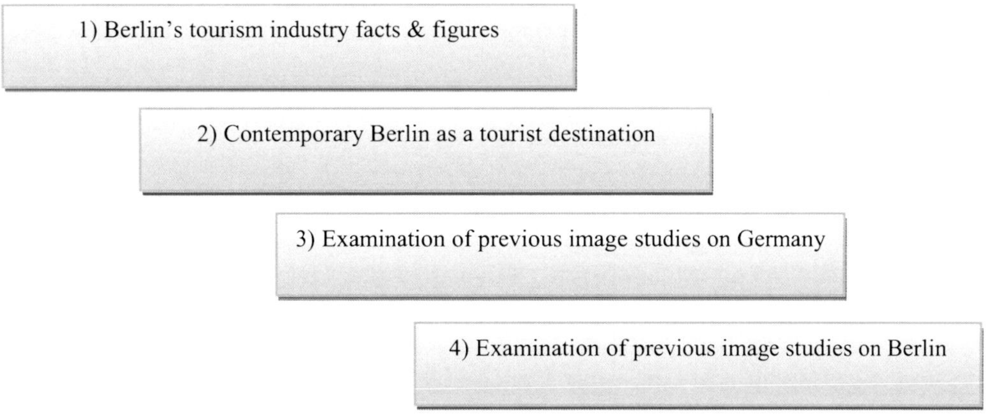

1) Berlin's tourism industry facts & figures

2) Contemporary Berlin as a tourist destination

3) Examination of previous image studies on Germany

4) Examination of previous image studies on Berlin

2.2 Berlin's tourism industry – facts and figures

Berlin is Germany's largest city with a population of 3.4 million people (BTM 2007). It is Germany's most visited city and increasingly becoming a popular tourist destination on an international scale. In 2007, Berlin counted 17.3 million bed nights and 7.6 million hotel guests, of whom 38.3% were foreign (BTM 2008a). This meant an immense rise for the fourth consecutive year and proves that Berlin is a popular city.

Germany is the most important source market for incoming tourists by number, followed by the UK, the US, Italy, the Netherlands and Spain (Table 2.1). In 2007, Berlin noted massive increases in hotel guests from the Baltic States [+ 57%], Ireland [+ 40.1%], Portugal [+35.5%] and Russia [+22%] (BTM 2008a). However, the number of Arab tourists was comparatively very small with only 40.551 overnight stays made, which meant a decrease of 0.9% on the previous year (BTM 2008b).

Table 2.1: Tourist arrivals in Berlin 2007

Markets	Overnight stays	Trend in %
Total	17.285.837	+8.6
Germany	10.671.866	+6.9
Total foreign	6.613.971	+11.6
UK	794.195	+6.4
Italy	589.009	+13.4
Netherlands	552.040	+10.6
Spain	544.133	+39.4
Denmark	390.470	+19.9
Middle East	40.551	-0.9

Source: BTM 2008b, Amt fuer Statistik Berlin-Brandenburg

Europe wide, Berlin is the 9th most visited city (Hedorfer 2008). What is striking though is that domestic tourists play a particularly high role in Berlin's tourism industry and represent about 65% of the total visitor numbers. Other European cities, even other German cities such as Frankfurt, Düsseldorf and Munich, have a much higher share of foreign tourists (+50%), which raises the question of whether Berlin has an image problem. Many English and Dutch, for example, still associate Germany with war (Smith-Spark 2006) and this might naturally have negative implications on Berlin and its tourism industry, as Germany's capital.

According to Nerger (cited BTM 2008a), the CEO of Berlin Tourismus Marketing GmbH, Berlin's aim is to reach 20 million bed nights by 2010. In order to reach this figure, an increased number of international visitors, including Arabs, would need to stimulate Berlin's tourism industry. Since tourists are believed to visit a destination only if they have a positive image of it (Prebensen 2007), it generally appears reasonable to study Berlin's image among foreigners. This project mainly studies the city's image among foreigners and might provide information, recommendations and alternatives to enhance the image if required.

2.3 Contemporary Berlin as a tourist destination

Travel guides (Lonely Planet 2008, Travel Smart 2008) indicate Berlin's attractiveness as a tourist destination. Germany's capital has undergone vast changes in the past decades and is a *'thriving, modern and exciting city'* at present (Travel Smart 2008) especially because of the large varieties of activities that appeal to visitors. The city has a lot to offer from cultural events, with numerous historical sites, multi-faceted architecture, brilliant shopping facilities, rich gastronomy and a vivid nightlife. Furthermore, Berlin is quite a green metropolis with 30% of the area covered by parks, lakes etc (BTM 2007). In particular Berlin's history and the city's importance during the Cold War, followed by the fall of the Berlin Wall, are of special interest for tourists.

Besides, Berlin is Germany's most multicultural city and approximately 14% of the population possess a foreign passport (BTM 2007). Most immigrants in Berlin are originally Turkish, so that some districts, such as Kreuzberg are even called 'Little Istanbul'.

The German stereotype is often considered as unfriendly; however, Berlin and its people differ in this regard. The capital is an amicable and tourist-friendly city according to a study on behalf of Reader's Digest (Strohmaier 2006) that compared 35 international metropolises in terms of friendliness, in which Berlin came fourth.

Despite Berlin's growing appeal and its tourism industry's positive development in recent years, a study conducted by the Swiss bank UBS (FAZ 2008) identified that Berlin is an inexpensive destination compared to other international cities. The city has a major competitive advantage by offering more economically priced lodging in the same hotel categories than many other European cities (Sueddeutsche 2007). Consequently, in conjunction with the destination attributes mentioned above, Berlin can be regarded as a highly attractive tourist place.

2.4 Examination of previous image studies on Germany

The events of the Second World War affect Germany's image even 60 years later. In some countries, Germany is still associated with features of the war (Geoghegan 2006) and, in the US and Russia, Hitler is the best-known German, for instance

(Deutsche Welle 2004). This casts a poor light on present day Germany and, arguably, on its tourism industry and may impinge on foreign people's image of the nation.

However, the FIFA World Cup 2006 in Germany induced positive implications on Germany as a tourist destination. Prior to the World Cup, a study of BPB (2005), the Federal Centre for Political Education, revealed that Germany's image was rather moderate in countries, such as the UK and Poland, for example, whereas Germany was already positively regarded in the Netherlands and Denmark. Yet, the World Cup further inspired Germany's image across other countries around the world. In the Anholt Nations Brand Index 2007 (see Appendix 2), which measures the image of countries by considering 6 factors namely tourism, people, culture and heritage, exports, governance and investment and immigration, Germany ranks first, which means a massive improvement over the previous couple of years (GNTB 2008, Hedorfer 2008). Germany could above all score high on tourism and exports as well as on culture and heritage; while, in terms of people, the score was rather low. However, it has overtaken countries, such as the UK, Italy, Canada and France which are well-established tourist destinations.

A further image study conducted by the BBC across 22 countries also revealed that Germany's political image was positive within the Western world; however, in Islamic-coined countries, such as Egypt and Turkey, the image was negative (cited Spiegel 2008). This might be the result of the political situation in the Middle East, because Arabs and other Islam members increasingly consider the Western world as an enemy (Galal *et al.* 2008). Galal *et al.* (2008) allege that, since 9/11, there have been many terrible waves between Arabs and Western people, mainly due to the political situation, which plays a major role in the Arab peoples' image of the West. Although Americans are considered as the main enemy, other Western countries are seen as allies, which might also affect Germany's image in Arabic nations.

Al-Hamarneh (2006) opposes this notion and claims that Germany has a good image in the Arab world for several reasons. Germany's anti-war policy during the Iraq crisis impressed Arabs and boosted Germany's bilateral relations with Arab nations (German Embassy 2008). Furthermore, 'Made in Germany' is highly appreciated, as it guarantees high quality. Germany is synonymous with high quality, which explains the nation's popularity for medical tourists from the Arab world (Al-Hamarneh 2006). However, Germans are also seen as hard-working, innovative, cultivated and helpful people and thus enjoy a good image too. Consequently, Germany seems to enjoy a positive position in the Arab world beyond the political situation.

2.5   Examination of previous image studies on Berlin

10 to 15 years ago, Berlin used to be a city in search of an identity, which projected a battered image, also as a result of huge economic problems (Focus 1994). Berlin has favourably managed its problems though and, nowadays, is one of Europe's most popular cities for tourists thanks to an image change, not only of Berlin but of Germany as a whole.

Although Berlin is still not mentioned in the same breath as Paris, New York or London (Adjouri 2008), it is increasingly perceived as international. For instance, the C&W/H&B's European Cities Monitor (cited Clark 2008), which ranks European cities by their business importance, repositioned Berlin on rank 8 in 2005, meaning an improvement of 7 places in comparison to 1990.

In addition, the Anholt City Brands Index 2005 (cited Clark 2008) ranks Berlin's brand-value within the top ten cities world-wide, which manifests Berlin's enhanced image. Nevertheless, as already mentioned above, Berlin is still not a big player among international cities, which is further visualised by the GAWC. GAWC (cited Clark 2008) clusters big cities in three different orders, Alpha, Beta and Gamma. Alpha-cities are defined as the most important world cities, Beta-cities are less significant and Gamma-cities are the least important. New York and London, for example, are Alpha-cities; whilst Berlin is a Gamma-city, which shows that, despite Berlin's recent success in tourism, the city might still not have a world reputation. While places such as London might induce clear images in people's minds around the world, Berlin's image might be more distorted the farther away people live from Berlin and this may affect primary research findings of this project. Some scholars (Prebensen 2007, Soenmez & Sirakaya 2002) assume that images of distant destinations are rather blurred, especially when the destination is not so known. In this regard, Protestant Europeans and Arabs might display varying images of Berlin, simply because the Arabs' image of the city could be blurred, especially where pre-visitation image is measured. As will be examined in 3.2, information sources are major influential factors in the image formation process. Since Berlin's marketing efforts are much higher in Europe than in the Arab world, the likelihood that people's picture of Berlin is clearer among Europeans than it is among Arabs is increased.

This is also likely regarding BTM's global marketing strategies. The further away the market is the more focus is put on strategic co-operations, which means Berlin is only represented by third parties in distant places (BTM 2006, p.18). BTM (2006, p.31) splits potential source markets into four different groups (Figure 2.2). Berlin allocates the highest marketing budget to primary markets, while the budget decreases gradually with the lowest budget for basic markets. Consequently, Berlin is much more involved in the UK market, than it is in the Middle East, for example, which might impinge on people's image of the city.

Figure 2.2: Ranking of markets in correspondence with their importance as source markets

Primary markets	Secondary markets	Growth markets	Base markets
1 Germany	5 France	15 Poland	Remaining markets
2 Great Britain	6 Italy	16 UAE/ Middle East	
3 USA	7 Switzerland	17 China	
4 The Netherlands	8 Japan	18 India	
	9 Russia		
	10 Austria		
	11 Spain		
	12 Sweden		
	13 Denmark		
	14 Norway		

Source: Berlin Tourismus, Berlin zum Erfolg 2006-2010, p.31

Previous image studies identified that Berlin's overall image is positive. Within its source markets (Germany, France, UK, Holland, Poland, and USA), Berlin is especially interesting due to its history, its sound accessibility, its cultural offer, its rich gastronomy and its vivid cityscape (Adjouri 2008, Habermann *et al.* 2006, Maschewski 2008a). The majority of the respondents also mention Berlin's sound shopping facilities, its multi-cultural ambiance and the great variety of activities as positive attributes, which create an overall pleasant atmosphere for tourists

(Habermann *et al.* 2008). Altogether, most respondents, including young tourists, perceive Berlin as a young, creative, multi-cultural, hospitable and dynamic city, while a small minority also mention interesting architecture as appealing (Adjouri 2008, Flatau 2008, Habermann *et al.* 2008, Karasek 2003, Maschewski 2008b). Only when considering the attributes of cleanliness and low price levels do a greater number of people disagree. What is more, many tourists are also disappointed to see little of the Berlin Wall remaining, having originally expected more (Maschewski 2008a).

Habermann *et al's* (2008) image study is appealing for this project, as it was based on about 2,000 respondents, of whom about 20% were under the age of 25. Furthermore, most of them were Germans, Dutch, Americans and British who are representative of Protestant Europe, except for the Americans who are also Protestants. This group exposed slight differences from elder groups in the perception of Berlin, albeit the image was also 'country of origin-specific'. For example, young people evaluated Berlin's friendliness of people and security issues lower than elderly people did, whereas older age groups gave smaller scores to cleanliness, but much higher ones in appreciating Berlin's numerous parks and other green areas (Habermann *et al.* 2006). Young people appreciated Berlin's lively nightlife in particular, whereas foreigners were more reserved than Germans. Differences also became apparent in terms of assessing friendliness since Italians evaluated this attribute lower than their counterparts. British and Italians assessed Berlin's price level as favourable, while Americans agreed to a lesser extent.

2.6 Summary

This chapter has introduced Berlin in various aspects of tourism. It has demonstrated that Berlin has undergone major changes in the last decades, which is why Berlin has become a thriving tourist destination. The capital is a modern city, which offers numerous appealing attributes for tourists. Partly, the success is also due to Germany's general change towards a positive image from which Berlin also seems to benefit. Regarding Habermann *et al's* image study, slight differences became obvious in the perception of Berlin as a tourist destination among different Protestant groups. In aggregate, these differences are too small though to derivate any significant resolutions, nonetheless, they might already indicate that greater differences may exist among varying cultural groups.

Chapter Three: Literature Review I

Destination Image

3.1 Introduction

This chapter focuses on an accurate analysis of what destination image is. Firstly, the term will be defined and its complexity exposed. Subsequent to this, the formation of destination image will be examined, as well as the factors that influence an individual's image formation. In the light of this study, destination image and the influence of cultural factors will be particularly analysed. Furthermore, this chapter presents an effective tool for measuring destination image. Figure 3.1 provides an overview.

Figure 3.1: Chapter overview

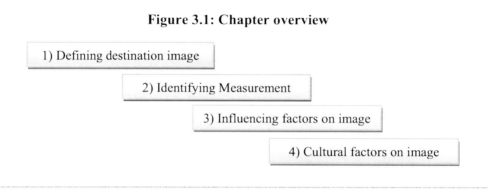

3.2 Defining destination image

Large ranges of marketing literature highlight the enormous importance of destination image (Cooper *et al. 2005,* Echtner & Brent Ritchie 2003, Frochot & Legohére 2007, p.176, Kim & Richardson 2003). The image of a place is a powerful and vital element in the decision of destination choice for a vacation (Page 2003, Cooper *et al.* 2005, Frochot & Legohére 2007, p.177). Some researchers consider destination image as the main factor *'in deciding where to travel'* (Chon 1990, Hunt 1975, Kent 1984, Colton 1987, Telisman-Kosuta 1989 cited Mac Kay & Fesenmaier 2000). Ateljevic (1999, p.193) even claims that image is regularly regarded *'to be more important than reality'*, as mental images form the basis of the holiday planning process and influence it accordingly.

Nevertheless, Chon (1989 cited Lubbe 2004) identifies a further influential factor in the destination selection process. According to him, two pivotal aspects generally motivate a tourist to travel. Firstly, the tourist recognises his or her needs and wants as travel objectives prior to assessing whether the destination can satisfy them.

Secondly, the tourist may have developed an image of the destination and consequently evaluates the extent to which the image matches the concept of their holiday. Jenkins (1999) adds a third point that influences a tourist's travel decision and claims that cognition and behaviour at the destination, as well as the level of satisfaction play a crucial role. Frochot and Legohere (2007, p.183) append that some people might just exclude a certain destination from their list of alternative places to visit, not because they have a negative image of the destination, but simply due to a lack of information and a basic lack of interest. Altogether, this demonstrates that destination image alone does not attract tourists.

Destination image is a vital aspect for destination managers yet it seems difficult to define the term precisely, since the term has been applied in a variety of contexts and disciplines in the past (Zhao 2006). Many researchers avoid an exact definition of it; Pearce (1988 cited Echtner & Brent Ritchie 2003), however, defined the term 'destination image' as follows:

> '...image is one of those terms that will not go away...a term with vague and shifting meanings'.

Hunt (1975) and Phelps (1986), on the other hand, consider destination image as:

> 'Perceptions held by potential visitors about an area'.

Both definitions expose how the term 'destination image' is being used in diverse contexts, although the latter definition is widely applied by most scholars (Crompton 1979, Tourism Canada 1986-1989, Gartner & Hunt 1987, Calantone *et al.* 1989 cited Echtner & Brent Ritchie 2003). Destination image is frequently summarised as a *'totality of impressions, beliefs, ideas, expectations, and feelings accumulated towards a place over time'* (Kim & Richardson 2003, Lubbe 2004). Coshall (2000) also believes in destination image being *'a series of perceptual beliefs, ideas and impressions of a destination'* which are influenced by several factors, such as past promotions, reputation, opinions of tour operators, and peer evaluation. This, in turn, shows that the difficulties in defining destination image might be due to the term's complexity, which is examined next.

3.2.1　　Destination image's complexity

The definitions mentioned in the previous section appear to be vague and inexplicit. Echtner and Brent Ritchie (2003) criticise that destination image is often purely explained as *'impressions of a place'* or *'perceptions of an area'*. The majority of researchers and their definitions merely consider destination image in terms of attributes and indicate unclear features regarding whether they include holistic or attribute-based components of image. Holistic components have recently gained more importance within the topic of destination image (Echtner & Brent Ritchie 2003).

For instance, Lubbe (2004) recognises that destination image is constructed of more than merely the attributes of a destination. He claims that a destination and an individual have a personal relationship, which stimulates the individual to create a particular picture of the destination and to assess whether the destination can fulfil his needs and expectations. Hence, the term 'destination image' is increasingly characterised by statements, such as *'the total impression a place makes on the mind of others'* (Reilly 1990 cited Echtner & Brent Ritchie 2003). According to Um and Crompton (1990 cited Echtner & Brent Ritchie 2003), destination image can be seen as a *'gestalt'* or a *'holistic construct'*. Pearce (1988, p.163) adds by signifying that the term 'destination image' often portrays *'an overall mental picture'*; nonetheless, each individual may perceive certain factors differently.

Beerli and Martin (2004) prove that destination image is a complex area of marketing. They state that most recent studies view destination image in consideration of two interrelated components. Firstly, perceptive/cognitive components relate to the individual's knowledge and beliefs of the place whilst, secondly, the individual also has an emotional interpretation of the place which reflects his feeling towards it. When both factors combine, they form a general destination image which will either be positive or negative (Baloglu & McCleary 1999). Stern and Krakover (1993 cited Beerli & Martin 2004) scientifically proved that affective components severely influence perceptive/cognitive components. Consequently, an individual's general feeling towards a place appears to be highly influential for the evaluation of other destination attributes.

Similarly, Beerli and Martin (2004) and Echtner and Brent Ritchie (2003) also interrelate two components concerning destination image, which they call attribute-based and holistic continuum. Attribute-based components are measurable characteristics, such as scenery, attractions, accommodation facilities and price levels, while holistic components rather consider intangible characteristics, such as friendliness, safety and atmosphere. Echtner and Brent Ritchie (2003) suggest that Martineau's notion of *'functional and psychological characteristics'* might be related to destination images in this context, since they play a crucial role in establishing the image of an entity. While functional characteristics are classified as *'directly observable or measurable'* (e.g. prices), psychological characteristics cannot be objectively measured (e.g. friendliness, atmosphere).

Figure 3.2: An illustrative example of the four components of destination image

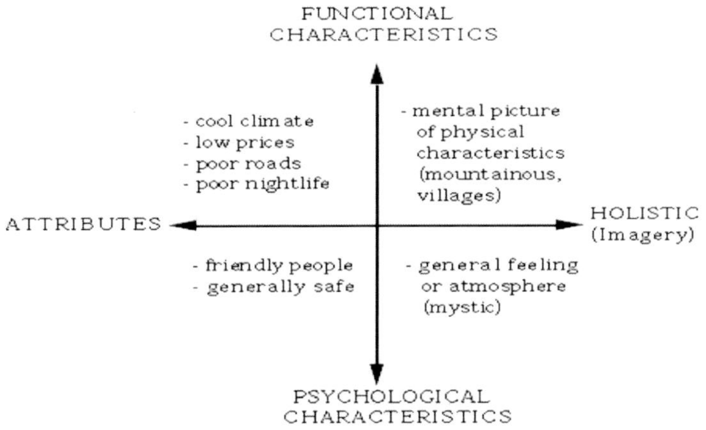

FUNCTIONAL
CHARACTERISTICS

- cool climate
- low prices
- poor roads
- poor nightlife

- mental picture
of physical
characteristics
(mountainous,
villages)

ATTRIBUTES

HOLISTIC
(Imagery)

- friendly people
- generally safe

- general feeling
or atmosphere
(mystic)

PSYCHOLOGICAL
CHARACTERISTICS

Source: The Journal of Tourism Studies 2003. 14 (1), p. 43

Echtner and Brent Ritchie (2003) propose the inclusion of these components in a measurement tool for image. Consequently, as shown in figure 3.2, to measure the perceptions of people towards a destination, consideration of the following attributes and characteristics is suggested:

➢ Individual functional attributes (e.g. price levels)
➢ Psychological attributes (e.g. friendliness)

> Functional holistic images, which originate from physical or measurable characteristics, such as a *'mental picture'* of a destination

> Psychological holistic images, which concern feelings about the overall impressions of the atmosphere.

Although the model seems to split perceived image into four influencing elements, Echtner and Brent Ritchie (2003) urge considering that the nature of the elements does not prevent overlaps between the four parts. As an example, they purport that holistic impressions are based on combinations and interactions of attributes whereas the perceptions of individual attributes may be influenced by overall impressions and feelings. Consequently, the separating line between psychological and functional characteristics is thin. Yet, this framework appears to provide a clear definition of destination image. Since Echtner and Brent Ritchie (2003) propose to apply the four components to measure destination image, they will form the foundation in the formulation of the questionnaire, which will be created for the purpose of primary research, concerning Arabs' and Protestants' image of Berlin (see Chapter 5).

Corresponding with the framework, destination image can be eventually defined as *'the holistic impression made by the destination'* and the perception of *'individual destination attributes'* (Echtner & Brent Ritchie 2003). However, how is a destination image formed? The succeeding section will examine this matter in more detail.

3.3   Destination image formation in the pre-visitation stage

Even though it is quite important for destination image developers to comprehend an individual's image formation process (Chon cited Zhao 2006), few empirical studies have been conducted in the past regarding forces that may influence an individual's image formation (Beerli & Martin 2004). Understanding how people form their image of places, however, enables destinations to be more competitive by raising their attractiveness where required.

Reynolds (1966 cited Zhao 2006) describes the formation of image as follows:

'The development of a mental construct based upon a few impressions chosen from a flood of information.'

The flood of information may consist of several sources comprising promotional literature, the general media and the opinion of others (Beerli & Martin 2004, Echtner & Brent Ritchie 2003, Frochot & Legohére 2007, p.178; Zhao 2006).

One's image of a destination depends on whether previous experience at the place exists or not, although Fakeye and Crompton (1991) contend the lack of empirical evidence regarding the implications of the visit on image. Still, Phelps (1986 cited Beerli & Martin 2004) differentiates between secondary and primary formed images. Primary image is developed by actually visiting the place, while secondary image relies on information sources. Various authors (Ateljevic 1999, p.198, Gartner & Hunt, Pearce & Phelps cited Beerli & Martin 2004) underline that primary image tends to be more rational and complex and thus differs from secondary image. Furthermore, the approaches of numerous studies (Baloglu & McCleary 1999, Beerli & Martin 2004, Echtner & Brent-Ritchie 2003, Vogt and Andereck 2003, Vogt and Stewart 1998) suggest divergences between the pre and post-visitation image, since they split both when measuring image. Therefore, several scholars (Di Marino 2007, Echtner & Brent Ritchie 2003, Hanlan & Kelly 2005, Kim & Richardson 2003) assert that when measuring image, it is advantageous to split the images of individuals that have already been to a place from those who have not, since modifications are possible in destination image before and after visitation.

In this context, Gunn (1988 cited Frochot & Legohére 2007, p.178) developed a model on the formation of image of the seven phases, which illustrates a constant building and alteration of images (Figure 3.3). It sub-divides the formation process into different phases and also indicates that images held by *potential visitors, non-visitors and returned visitors'* might vary. Since it is suggested that their images are split when destination image is measured, this study's primary research will focus on surveying youths that have never visited Berlin. Besides, the pre-visitation image is highly influential on an individual's decision to visit a place (Zhao 2006).

Figure 3.3: Gunn's Seven Phases Model

1. Accumulation of mental images about vacation experiences
2. Modification of those images by further information
3. Decision to take a vacation trip
4. Travel to the destination
5. Participation at the destination
6. Return home
7. Modification of images based on the vacation experience

Source: The Journal of Tourism 2003. 14 (1), p. 37

Within the model, Frochot and Legohére (2007, p.178) discover three different levels or phases. Phases 1 to 3 are *'pre-visitation stages'*, 4 and 5 *'during-visitation stages'* and stages 6 and 7 are *'post-visitation stages'*. The focus of this study is on the pre-visitation stage, so the other stages will not be examined in detail.

An individual's image in phases 1 and 2 relies on secondary sources of information. Between the pre-visitation stages relevant differences exist whereas, in phase 1, an individual has an organic type of image and, in phase 2, it is an induced one. Cooper *et al.* (2005, p.63) define 'organic image' as *'the sum of all information that has not been deliberately directed by advertising or promotion of a country or destination'*. This information is generally gathered from non-touristic or non-commercial sources, such as magazines, newspapers, education and the opinions of friends and family (Echtner & Brent Ritchie 2003). According to Frochot and Legohére (2007, p.178) this phase is quite influential; since individuals may unconsciously develop a rigid opinion of the place throughout their life, before the place is even considered as a holiday destination. Cooper *et al.* (2005:63-64) describe the first phase as a vague and fantasy type of image. At this phase, destination marketers have the least influence on potential visitors, since mental images are built continuously, affected by daily news and other information sources, which do not necessarily have to be connected to tourism, but may still affect one's image of a tourist destination.

The level of influence destination marketers have on an individual's image changes in phase 2 when they can deliberately promote their products by such means as 'educational tours' and PR, in order to raise awareness and inform potential visitors of the product (Cooper *et al.* 2005, p.63, Frochot & Legohére 2007, p.179). Once an individual decides to go on holiday, he or she will inspect several destinations for which additional information might be collected. It is at phase 2, where destinations have to be particularly creative in order to attract tourists. Nevertheless, this becomes easier the more positive the overall image of the destination is, meaning that it is vital that a destination promotes itself well.

Generally, it appears that an induced image is more controllable, while an organic image is more difficult to be influenced (Cooper *et al.* 2005:63). Although several sources claim the superiority of the organically formed image (Beerli & Martin 2004, Cathy *et al.* 2004, Cooper *et al.* 2005, p.63, Zhao 2006), Frochot and Legohére (2007, p.179-180) clarify that this may change at certain points. They signify that the further away the potential visitor lives, the more likely it is that the induced type of image becomes more influential, as he/she would consider external information sources, as more credible and more reliable than their own mental picture of a place.

This section presented the image formation process of a place in the pre-visitation stage without looking at influencing factors in depth. The following section enumerates various factors that have an effect on the image formation process.

3.4 Factors influencing the formation of pre-visitation destination image

Various factors influence the image formation process. Baloglu and McCleary (1999) suggest a general framework of destination image formation that distinguishes between stimulus factors and personal factors, which are both influential on one's image formation (Figure 3.4). They argue that these factors primarily cause and form image. While stimulus factors arise from external sources, personal factors illustrate individual characteristics.

Information sources are considered as stimulus factors (Baloglu & McCleary 1999) or as image forming agents, according to Gartner's model of the eight-image forming agents (Gartner 1993). Plenty of studies (Fakeye & Crompton 1991, Gartner 1993, Mansfeld 1992, Um & Crompton 1990, Woodside & Lysonsky 1989 cited Beerli & Martin 2004) ascertain that information sources, together with the factors mentioned in the framework, determine one's destination choice. Depending on the quantity and the miscellaneous character of the information, people will be either influenced to consider a certain destination to travel to or not.

Figure 3.4: A General Framework of Destination Image Formation

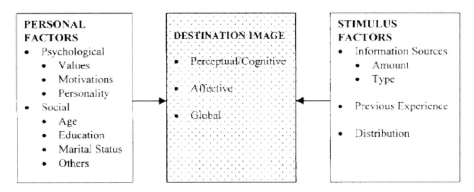

Source: Annals of Tourism Research 1999. 25 (4), p. 870

Various information sources will then independently form a single image in people's minds (Gartner 1993). Gartner (1993) supposes that this information is in its nature 'overt induced' (e.g. conventional advertising in the mass media), 'covert induced' (e.g. destination reports or articles), 'autonomous' (e.g. mass-media broadcasting news or documentaries) and 'organic' (e.g. information from friends and relatives). Hanley and Kelly (2005) also state that image formation development is subject to a multi-stage process where travellers are exposed to information sources that are partly beyond the control of destination authorities, which once again shows the subject's complexity.

What is more, previous personal experience affects the individual's image of a place. Beerli and Martin (2004) define personal experience as *'the intensity of the visit' to a place;* however, this study focuses on destination image in the pre-visitation stage and will thus only consider influential pre-visitation factors. Yet, an interesting assertion is made in this context. Individuals' motivations and interests differ from one person to another and may affect the image of a place (Baloglu & McCleary 1999, Tasci 2007). While one person may be interested in cultural city tourism, another may prefer beach tourism, for example. Consequently, the first one would most likely be more inclined to construct a favourable image of Berlin, since it meets his interests. Um and Crompton (1990 cited Beerli & Martin 2004) concur with this assumption and add that the image will be developed in accordance with the *image projected by the destination and the individual's own needs, motivations, prior knowledge, preferences, and other personal characteristics'*. Hence, the perception of a place may vary among individuals, depending on personal preferences.

Baloglu and McCleary's framework of destination image formation (Figure 3.4) may entail weaknesses, as explained in the following. In a previous study, Baloglu (1997 cited Beerli & Martin 2004) identified that socio-demographic differences among people did not result in different perceptions of a place. Other sources (Baloglu & McCleary 1999, Stern & Krakover 1993) support his view by claiming that the level of socio-demographic influence is low. Beerli and Martin (2004) examined this issue in depth. They deduced that the factors age, education and social class only partially showed any significant relationship with the perceived image, while the factors gender and country of origin clearly stood in connection with it.

Nonetheless, Baloglu and McCleary's framework also gets backing regarding the influence of socio-demographic characteristics. Stabler (1995) proposes that personal characteristics, such as age, gender, education, marital status and social class are 'internal inputs' that affect one's view of a place. Thus, concerning this study's primary research and sample, socio-demographic characteristics will be considered by focussing on youth survey participants (see Chapter 5). Such a method seems to make collected data more comparable.

What becomes evident by scrutinising the topic of destination image is the low number of studies that incorporate cultural factors in the image formation process. In separate studies, Newman (2004) and Tasci (2007) found that various ethnic or even racial groups within one country vary in their perception of objects. Furthermore, they claim that cultural factors determine whether certain objects are appealing to an individual or not.

In general, cultural aspects are acquiring importance within the tourism industry (Birkeland & Isaksen 2007) and will increasingly impinge on how tourism organisations will have to work in the future. The international tourism industry is becoming increasingly globalised which makes it imperative for destination managers to comprehend cultural norms and their repercussion on tourism behaviour (Kee-Fu Tsang & Ap 2007). Thus, cultural factors will be further examined in the following section.

3.5   Cultural factors influencing destination image formation

The image formation process is claimed to be culture-specific. Truong and King (2006) argue that perception is an important component of culture. Samovar and Porter (1991 cited Truong & King 2006) alternatively consider culture as a major determinant of perception, which extensively influences the way objects or experiences are perceived. Thus, it is argued that the image formation process is *'culturally determined'*. Various literatures point out that a significant relationship exists among culture and perceptions (Truong & King 2006). Since destination image plays an important part in a tourist's buying behaviour of a vacation, it will be vital to examine the implications of culture on the image formation process in more detail.

Some prior culture-based tourism studies (Kang & Moscardo 2006, Murphy 2003, Srnka 2007, van Egmond 2005) showed that tourists from different countries differ in their behaviour, as a result of cultural disparities. Additionally, in terms of perception, cultural differences have been identified. You *et al.* (2000 cited Zhao 2006) highlight that people from different cultural backgrounds perceive the same objects and holiday experiences differently. Generally, they regard tourism as *'culture-specific'*, as tourism is becoming ever more globalised with tourists from a vast number of cultural backgrounds. A study conducted by Kozak *et al.* (2004) demonstrates that, in the image formation process, significant differences existed among people from a variety of cultural backgrounds. Several other scholars (Ateljevic 1999, p.199, Beerli & Martin 2004, Frochot & Legohere 2007, p.184, Kee-Fu Tsang & Ap 2007, MacKay & Fesenmaier 2000, Mattila 2000, Reisinger & Turner 2002a, Truong & King 2006, Zhao 2006) support Kozak *et al's* (2004) findings by having carried out similar studies on a wide range of nationalities with comparable results.

Cooper *et al.* (2005, p.63) add that a society is characterised by sharing similar lifestyles. Consequently, people from the same society show numerous similarities in their travel behaviour, whereas another society may be coined by a diverse lifestyle and, hence, is different. Frochot and Legohere (2007, p.184) believe that disparities are present due to distinctions in history, and traditions and values of cultures, so that divergences in the perception of destinations come unsurprisingly. Relph (1976 cited Lubbe 2004) realises that *'individual images are constantly being socialised through the use of common languages, symbols and experiences'*, which means that individuals' perceptual beliefs are affected by their daily environment. Hence, different cultural groups develop communities that differ fundamentally from each other in their beliefs etc. Zhao (2006) enumerates three more causes for cultural differences:

- ➢ Geographical location, which means that culture is place-specific
- ➢ The concept of 'cultural distance'
- ➢ Personal values.

Other previous studies (Baloglu *et al.* 2004, Ahmed 1991, Crompton 1979, Douglas 1977, Gartner & Hunt 1987 cited Zhao 2006, Font 1996, Reisinger & Turner 2003, p.153) went into more detail about culture and its relation to destination image. They emphasised their findings of contrasting images for the same destination among people from different regions. Contiguous to cultural factors being influential, the way tourists receive information about a destination also plays a major role (Blackwell *et al.* 2001 cited Zhao 2006). People that live further away will naturally receive less information about a certain place than others that live closer; this phenomenon is called *'distance factor'* (Blackwell *et al.* 2001 cited Zhao 2006, Frochot & Legohere 2007, p.184). However, the nature of 'differently perceived image' is not restricted to national borders (Frochot & Legohere 2007, p.185). Ahmed (1991 cited Zhao 2006) and Zhao (2006) carried out studies showing that people from the same country but different regions, can show dissimilarities in the perception of places. In summary, it can be assumed that people living closer to a certain place develop more realistic and complex images than people from further away, as they might have more contact with the destination.

The concept of 'cultural distance' relates to the degree to which the destination's culture varies from the visitor's home culture (McIntosh & Goeldner 1990 cited Zhao 2006). They suggest that tourists from further away are more likely to visit a destination due to its cultural offerings in order to satisfy their hunger for experiencing a new culture, than tourists living nearby. Consequently, they come to know a destination from an altered perspective. As an example, this would mean that a Dutch person visiting Berlin might perceive the city differently from an Arab due to diverse intentions of their visit.

A further crucial factor relating to culture is the factor of personal values. A personal value is defined as a compound of attitudes, knowledge, abilities and values that notably impinges on an individual's actions in the course of his/her life (Vinson *et al.* 1977). Personal values underlie a life-long learning process, in which the culture of the home country has a great influence. Due to diverse development of cultures, these personal values fluctuate from culture to culture. Since, personal value systems influence people's lifestyles, they might also impact on people's tourist behaviour and, as a consequence, on how destinations are perceived (Madrigal & Kahle 1994). Truong and King (2006) add that it is unsurprising that destination image perceptions differ, *'given that worldviews are very diverse'*.

Although a large number of scholars propose that destination image is culture-specific, there are also some voices that claim the opposite or question the influence of cultural factors on the perceived image of objects and places. In a study of 'India's Destination Image', Chaudary (2000) found no significant cultural disparities in the way that British, Dutch and Germans perceived India. Consequently, the assumption that people from different countries vary in their perception of objects can be questioned. However, Inglehart *et al.* (cited van Egmond 2005, p.6-7) argues that one should rather distinguish between protestant countries and catholic countries (see 1.4.1 & Appendix 1) that show remarkable cultural differences among each other, whereas, within their cultural background, they demonstrate similarities. Therefore, Chaudary's findings might be unsurprising and support Inglehart *et al*'s point of view, since they show that tourists from traditionally protestant countries unveil behavioural similarities. It is arguably more surprising that MacKay and Fesenmaier (2000) only found some moderate differences in the perception of certain destination attributes among Taiwanese and American students in one of their studies. Other sources (Dann 1993, Plog 1990 cited Kozak *et* al. 2003) criticise cross-cultural studies in tourism and claim that globalisation of the tourist phenomenon permits a better understanding of the global tourist. Yet, it has to be considered that MacKay and Fesenmaier only conducted an exploratory study with a small sample, which means the finding's significance can be contested.

Matsumoto *et al.* (2001) generally criticise a wide range of cross-cultural studies carried out on this topic. Especially, the measurements employed to identify perceived image differences or similarities among groups do not lead to reliable results, so it cannot be ensured that cultural differences really exist (Matsumoto *et al.* 2001). Hence, it remains doubtful whether differences in the answers of interviewees really connote that people are different.

Potentially, MacKay and Fesenmaier's findings demonstrate that the on-going globalisation process may induce more homogenous lifestyles between different cultures, but contradicting sources claim that culture influences one's behaviour. In this context, it is one of this study's objectives to find an answer. Consequently, the author of this study will put much emphasis on applying appropriate research methods that increase the likelihood of achieving relevant results.

3.6   Summary

This section unveiled the multi-faceted nature of destination image. It is a very complex area of marketing due to various factors that influence one's image of a place. Not only does a destination's attributes determine the image of the place but individual's also have a personal relationship with a place meaning that destination image depends on attribute-based and holistic components.

Furthermore, the implications of stimulus and personal factors were scrutinised and demonstrated the influential role of information sources and socio-demographic factors on destination image. Subsequently, the effects of cultural factors were analysed, which identified that cultural factors seem to determine one's image of a place, although there are also opponents of this proposition. They purport that, in the era of globalisation, tourist behaviour is becoming more homogenous, which permits a better understanding of the global tourist. Consequently, the effect of culture on destination image remains controversial.

The next chapter goes into more detail concerning the effects of globalisation on consumer behaviour and analyses whether globalisation is globally precipitating more homogenous consumer behaviour. It also examines and compares the Arab-Islamic and Protestant-European culture with particular emphasis on the respective youth cultures, so that this point can contribute to finding an answer to the question mentioned above.

Chapter Four: Literature Review II

Globalisation: Its effects on consumer

behaviour. Comparing Arab-Islamic

and Protestant European Culture.

4.1   Introduction

This chapter investigates the effects of globalisation on consumer behaviour and whether it globally induces more homogenous consumer behaviour. The Arab-Islamic and Protestant European culture, particularly youth cultures, are examined and compared to identify potential effects of globalisation. Finally, this chapter summarises the literature review and demonstrates the research gap. Figure 4.1 provides an overview.

Figure 4.1: Chapter overview

1) Influence of globalisation on consumer behaviour

2) Analysis: Arab-Islamic and Protestant European cultures

3) Arab-Islamic and Protestant European youth cultures

4) Summary

5) Literature review: conclusions and research gap

4.2   The influence of globalisation on consumer behaviour

Globalisation concerns the larger *'interconnectedness'* between the world's people, not only in economic terms, but also the political, social and cultural elements (Eitzen & Baca Zinn 2006, p.1). Eitzen and Baca Zinn (2006, p.1) add that globalisation incorporates a variety of processes in which *'goods, information, people, money, communication, and fashion (and other forms of culture) move across national boundaries'*. Waters (2001, p.5) defines as follows:

> *'A social process in which the constraints of geography on economic, political, social and cultural arrangements recede, in which people become increasingly aware that they are receding and in which people act accordingly'.*

Hence, it is often presumed that globalisation effects could create more homogenous consumer behaviour among varying cultures; however, this notion is debatable (Suh & Kwon 2002). In fact conflicting sources exist with one side supporting the theory of the global consumer and the development of a more homogenous market (Abi-Saab 2005, Friedman 2005, Levitt 1983, Waters 2001, p.5), while the other opposes the theory (de Moiji 2004, p.46, Frost 2006, Halter 1995, p.109, Naisbitt 1994, p.253, Rifkin 2001, Sharma *et al.* 1994, Suh & Kwon 2002, Schuette & Ciarlante cited Wirtz 2001).

The proposition that globalisation homogenises buying behaviour across countries does not underlie any empirical evidence (Belk 1996). Still, Schuette and Ciarlante (1998 cited Suh & Kwon 2002) claim that globalisation can lead to increasing people's sensitivity towards other cultures and values, with possible impacts on their consumer behaviour. Waters (2001, p.5) adds that this globalised world is coined by a single society and culture, still with variations, but territoriality will vanish as an organising principle for social and cultural life.

Fukuyama (1998) concurs with him, but on a different level. He argues that cultures are becoming more homogenous, merely concerning large economic and political institutions. Yet, he admits that it may subsequently influence culture at lower levels, although he generally believes that globalisation does not homogenise cultures, instead he recognises the reverse effects of globalisation, referred to later. Levitt (1983) is much more convinced of world homogenisation from globalisation and affirms that cultural differences are remains of the past. People's preferences and tastes increasingly assimilate across the world, which is also partly due to multi-national organisations. Levitt's notion in 1983 may be regarded as obsolete, yet a more recent study (Keillor *et al.* 2001 cited Suh & Kwon 2002) found that consumers decreasingly attach ethnocentric tendencies to their buying behaviour on a global scale, which could mean that consumers' buying behaviour increasingly resembles global. Especially, younger people are considered to be more susceptible to the effects of globalisation mainly thanks to the internet (Abi-Saab 2005, Inglehart 1997, p.19). What becomes clear is that most scholars that claim homogenising effects for globalisation are originally American. Keeping America's history in mind, which was predominantly marked by successful integration of people from various cultural backgrounds, it appears that Americans believe that their success can be extended and adopted globally, which may cause a biased stance.

Hence, their assumptions confront various counter-arguments. Naisbitt (1994, p.255) claims that the traditional nation-state has weakened as a consequence of global economic and technological forces, yet these forces have strengthened certain cultures, religions and ethnic heritages. Various sources purport that globalisation achieves the contrary of homogenisation and refer to invigoration and revitalisation of culture, which can also induce more patriotic consumer behaviour (Abi-Saab 2005, Djursaa & Kragh 1997, Fukuyama 1998, Ritzer 2003, Waters 2001, p.3). Inglehart (1997, p.23) talks of postmodernism, which is a reaction to modernisation and a rejection of Westernisation. Postmodernism incorporates greater tolerance for other cultures, yet own traditions and cultural values are revalorised. This further impinges on people's consumer behaviour, which becomes more patriotic (Ritzer 2003, Sharma *et al.* 1994, Suh & Kwon 2002). For instance, Suh and Kwon (2002) identify that, even among US citizens, consumer ethnocentrism is quite significant despite the immense wave of globalisation, which Americans actually commenced (Sbragia 2007). Growing animosity among certain cultures appears to be considerably influential in this respect. For instance, Suh and Kwon (2002) argue that Koreans are reluctant to purchase Japanese products due to negative relationships in the past. Nowadays, hostility between the Western world and the Arab world may thus affect Arab consumer behaviour too. Fundamental resistance is partly the answer to Westernisation in the Arab world (Abi-Saab 2005, Waters 2001, p.3) and, consequently, growing numbers of Arabs boycott American products, for example (Fasman 2003, Pallister 2003).

Today's world appears shaken with conflicts and wars, so the assumption of a generally more homogenous world hardly seems reasonable, as most conflicts (Tibet and China and Palestine-Israel conflict e.g.) are based on cultural grounds. Since animosity impinges on consumer behaviour, reverse effects of globalisation are almost apparent. So, why are there contradicting propositions about the effects of globalisation? Suh and Kwon (2002) enumerate a simple reason; *'the implications of globalisation vary culture by culture'.* The idea 'globalisation leads to homogenisation' appears to be an ethnocentric point of view of Western countries, which cannot be shared concerning the rest of the world.

In this regard, the following section examines the Arab-Islamic and Protestant European culture in order to identify potential differences and similarities.

4.3 Analysis: Arab-Islamic and Protestant European cultures

In order to understand potential cultural differences or similarities in consumer behaviour among both cultures, it might be useful to understand general cultural aspects first, which are portrayed in figure 4.2.

Arab-Islamic culture fundamentally differs from Western culture. The Islam is the source of Arabic culture and Arabic language (Altawajiri 1998, Mansfield 2003, p.14-17), whereas Western culture depicts on Greek notions, Roman law, the Latin language and Christian expectations (Brooklyn College 1999, Halsall 1998, Lashbrook 1969). Consequently, both cultures have developed diversely, although they demonstrate some similarities, as shown within this section.

Figure 4.2: Arab perspective vs. Western perspective

Arab	Western
➢ Family - Center of everything. (Father has first and last word).	➢ Family – Important but not as central to individual.
➢ Friends – Periphery, but courteous to all.	➢ Friends – Core to some, important to most.
➢ Honor – Very important amongst Arabs. Honor will be protected and defended at all costs.	➢ Honor – Typically not as important.
➢ Shame (especially against family) – avoided at all costs, insults and criticism are taken very seriously.	➢ Shame – Typically not as important.
➢ Religion – Central to all things.	➢ Religion – Varies by individual, very personal, not discussed in polite conversation.
➢ Society – Family/tribe is most important.	➢ Society – Individual rights.
➢ Government – Most governments are secular, but still emphasize religion.	➢ Government – Purpose is to protect rights and improve standard of living.
➢ Age and Wisdom honoured.	➢ Youth and Beauty praised.
➢ Wealth honored in both cultures.	➢ Wealth honored in both cultures.

Source: US Army (2006)

Arab culture is severely influenced by the Islam which is a cornerstone in Arabs' belief and way of life (Altawajiri 1998, Al-Wugayan 2004). Since the Islam is not only seen as a religion but also as a program of life, the Arab's general behaviour is closely linked with the following Islamic characteristics:

'Universality, inclusiveness, moderation, realism, objectivity, and diversity in unity'.

Furthermore, the Islam is the reference for the search of truths in respect of values, existence, reality and behaviour (Altawajiri 1998). What is also quite important to understand in relation to tourism is that the Holy Qur'an is indicatory for moral and social teachings. As a consequence, the hedonistic lifestyle of the Western world might widely be considered as nearly rebellious and deterring; hence, Arabs often prefer travelling within the Arab world (Mintel 2006b). However, this might have changed among younger generations of Arabs and will be further examined in 4.4.

Despite the aversion towards the Western world's hedonistic life style, the Islamic culture is a broad-minded culture that advocates the gain of knowledge, dialogue and coexistence, which might not always be applicable for all Arab people, but to the majority. What has to be considered is that the Arab world consists of numerous countries that might slightly differ regarding certain cultural aspects. In spite of the diversity, it is acknowledged that there is an affirmed unity and harmony among the Arab world (ISESCO 2008). The Arab culture is characterised by an over-proportionally strong togetherness that Hofstede (cited Buda 1998) and Al-Wugayan (2004) describe as collectivist, which is associated with homogenous cultures (Tang & Koveos 2008). The family is one of the most important components of Arab life and also reflects in Arabs' propensity to travel in large groups.

The collectivistic nature of the Arab world also precipitates certain Arab values, which notably vary from Western stereotypes (Emery 2008). Essential features of Arabs' behaviour are *'hospitality, generosity, good manners, loyalty, honour, reputation, respect for elders, love and unconditional support of family and friends'*. Some of these traits also play a role in Western cultures, albeit it is acknowledged that they are more individualistic and less influenced by them (Al-Wugayan 2004, Emery 2008, van Egmond 2005, p.20).

In this respect some similarities emerge, which is unsurprising considering that the holy bible, which influences most parts of the Western world, including traditionally Protestant countries, and the holy Qur'an share the same roots, many prophets and worship the same god, although each group calls its God by a different name (Emery 2008, Kateregga and Shenk 1997, p.1-7). Consequently, the Arab-Islamic and Protestant European cultures share some basic values.

Both cultures embody the tradition of ascetic abstinence in which all forms of excessive self-indulgence are forbidden (Al-Wugayan 2004, US Army 2006, van Egmond 2005, p.18). Concerning this, self-discipline is crucial, which is conducive to the sacrifice of excessive enjoyment. Empathy for the weak is additionally considered as one of the key pillars. Caring for each other and having warm relations between people outline these cultures. However, these elements are weaker within the Protestant society, which may partly be a consequence of the drastic drop-off in church attendance in the Western world (Knox 2005). Plummeting church attendance might bring about negligence of certain moral norms among the population. Surprisingly though, despite a fundamentalist movement in the Arab world, mosque attendance is also dropping in some Arab countries, principally among younger Arabs (Maussen 2005, Zia-Ebrahimi 2005). This may be symbolic of secularisation, as young Muslims distance themselves from *'the Islam of the fathers',* which did not deal with alien environments, in the quest to improve coexistence with global counterparts (Roy cited Maussen 2005). As a result, this may prompt young Arabs to absorb more Western lifestyles and values, so that similarities might gradually emerge more among these cultures.

Furthermore, the Arab-Islamic and Protestant cultures apply strong moral standards. Strong egalitarianism characterises the Protestant- as well as the Islamic ideal, although the latter has been modified and exploited by many past Arab leaders by living as monarchies, whereas Protestants have been living 'democracy' (Saeed 2004, Van Egmond 2005, p.19). These government forms naturally shape their population. Since they vary from each other in composition and execution, it must be assumed that people develop different lifestyles too.

Table 4.1: Hofstede's Cultural Indices

Arab World	Protestant countries
High power distance	Low power distance
High collectivism	High Individualism
High masculinity index	Low masculinity index
High uncertainty avoidance	Low uncertainty avoidance

Source: Hofstede (2003)

Hofstede's Cultural Dimensions demonstrates large cultural differences among Arabs and Protestant Europeans (Table 4.1). He clearly deduces cultural differences between the Arab world and countries with a Protestant history and all the indices in table 4.1 demonstrate significant differences between the groups (Hofstede 2003). The Arab world's large power distance contradicts the Islamic ideal like the high masculinity index though and Saeed (2004) emphasises that this phenomena has only taken place due to numerous influential men in Arab history that exploited the Islam in order to be superior to women. The Arab youth movement away from the parents' ideal could derail Arab monarchies and, simultaneously, the superior role of Arab men, as erode the gap between Arab and Western forms of government, which could also impact on the population and their lifestyle.

Some sources support the latter proposition. Hofstede has arguably conducted the most comprehensive cultural studies; nonetheless, according to At-Twaijri and Al-Muhaiza (2004), it disregards possible changes over time. They claim that countries change and that cultural values may underlie a constantly developing process in which modifications are possible. Their study identified some fluctuations to Hofstede's findings on the Arab world in terms of collectivism, the masculinity index and power distance, which have all weakened and might change more in accordance with the Western world. According to Perry (2006), a university professor in Michigan, the Arab world is increasingly becoming more susceptible to being influenced by American mass-media stereotypes, which is also accelerated by globalisation. Consequently, Arab culture is changing and more Western values are absorbed, especially among youths who are more proficient with contemporary mass-media, such as the Internet.

In tourism, certain indications may also demonstrate a change in Arabs' attitudes, which seemingly become more aligned with certain Western behavioural patterns. For example, excessive pleasure, which has long been a taboo in the Arab world, is becoming increasingly a trend, especially among the younger generation. Several sources and blogs talk about growing numbers of Arabs taking part in sex tourism, which some sources (Cherkaoui 2007, El-Gawhary 1995, ETN 2008) consider an effect of globalisation, attracting people to what is perceived as exotic. According to Usher (2007), a generation gap is evermore forming in the Middle East, in which the youth population is searching for its own identity, which progressively resembles Western lifestyles whilst, simultaneously, ignoring particular Islamic values. In this context, the possible implications of globalisation are in evidence.

The following section will look at the eventual transformation process of Arab youths in more detail and examine Arab youths' changing attitude compared to Protestant youth culture

4.4   Arab-Islamic and Protestant European youth cultures

Unsurprisingly, basic Arab-Islamic values (Figure 4.2) also impinge on Arab youths: however, according to Rayappa (2005), Senior Account Manager of TNS Middle East & Africa, and Al Lawati *et al.* (2007) the young population of the region is in search of a new identity in an attempt to approach the rest of the world. This transformation process is challenging long held beliefs in character, whilst maintaining a distinct identity on the one hand and reaching at the possibility *'to be part of the global community that the new media freedoms and frankness presents'* on the other (Rayappa 2005).

Within the Arab world, young people are becoming a vitally influential part, since they represent the fastest growing segment of the Arab population with 60% of the region being under 30 years of age and 50% under 25 years of age, which make these societies 'youthful' (Al-Ghanim 2005, Gavlak 2008, UNESCO 2006). Thus, the transformation movement has to be taken seriously. These societies increasingly embody modern life and are connected to the world by having access to satellite TV, internet, cell phones, and higher education, which are dimensions former generations never knew (Rayappa 2005).

Why is the Arab world's youth going through a transformation process? Various sources claim that the soaring unemployment rate among the young population mobilises such a process (Al-Ghanim 2005, Rayappa 2005). According to a survey of the UN (2001 cited Al-Ghanim 2005), over 51% of Arab youth contemplate emigrating to a Western State to pursue a better lifestyle and equal opportunities for jobs, which demonstrates their present dissatisfaction. Many bemoan the missed opportunities of their parents to create a better life, despite an 'era of oil'. They believe it is time to move on and to learn from their global counterparts: hence, their way of thinking and behaving is considerably altering, channelled by the search for a modern lifestyle and merging Western aspects, yet without neglecting the core of their own culture and tradition (Rayappa 2005). They want all the freedom that Western counterparts enjoy, but embedded in Islamic values.

A research project conducted by Rayappa (2005) deduced that Arab youths want to become part of a global youth culture.

> *'Unabashed consumerism, a passion for technology, a need to have fun, hope and trust in what the future might hold, self-confidence and a sense of identity, wanting to make the world a better place to live, and an awareness and respect for global icons'.*

From this it emerges that contemporary Arab youths share similar goals with the Western world, which will be shown subsequently.

Protestant Europe also appears to be within a transformation process due to a youth movement (Keller & Stewart 2005, p.63). Bell (1987) claims that Protestant youth culture is suffering a fractured ethnic identity, characterised by wide-ranging dissonances with traditional parental values. There is a shift away from church and culture among protestant youths, progressing towards a love for nature, which almost recalls the era of romanticism and leads to a new conception of the universe (Keller & Stewart 2005, p.69). It seems that Protestant belief plays a minor part in their conception and that they follow the ideal of a unified world, in which felt fellowship is more important than Protestant individualism. More emphasis is quasi put upon raising the awareness of common responsibilities for the world and promoting personal liberty on a global scale, than on traditional values. Consequently, only 7% of Protestant youths go to church (Bertelsmann 2008), which illustrates the secondary role of religion.

Protestant youths are nevertheless shaped by protestant values according to Dr. Feldmann (cited Black 2007). Protestantism incorporates hard work, which is transmitted to youths through public institutions, such as schools. He argues that this work ethic still distinguishes Protestants from people from other societies, for example, Muslims. The strong work ethic is also conducive to the strong position of women in the labour environment and generally in society, which extremely differs from women's position in Arabic countries. In this context, the implications on tourism need to be stated. While women from Protestant Europe can freely travel, women from Islamic countries only travel in the presence of a male family member and this attitude is still prevalent.

However, in another aspect, Arab youths and Protestant youths seem to be similar, both are facing problematic situations that may induce structural changes to their societies. Arab youths face the problem of high unemployment, which almost forces them to consider cultural modifications for the pursuit of a better life, as cultural constraints often hinder the Arab world's development in economic terms. Protestant youths, however, face problems on a cultural and moral level (Tucker 2000), since moral conscience is incrementally decreasing, not only among Protestants but generally within Western culture (Benedict XVI 2006).

4.5   Summary

This chapter has demonstrated that globalisation generally affects consumer behaviour. However, several scholars tend to suggest that globalisation does not homogenise consumer behaviour, but rather causes reverse effects, such as increased consumer-ethnocentrism. Consequently, it could be summarised that despite the massive wave of globalisation, cultures are fundamentally still different in their tastes and preferences, if not even more different.

This may change though, since younger generations are more susceptible to the effects of globalisation, as the analysis of the Arab-Islamic and Protestant European youth culture has shown. The cultures are fundamentally different since, although they share certain values, they implement them to varying extents. The Arab youth culture is changing as it attempts to absorb more Western values in the pursuit for a better life without abandoning core Islamic values. It could be established that Protestant European youth culture is also experiencing a transformation process. Both youth groups are striving for a better life with Arabs intending to improve communication with the Western World, while youths from Protestant Europe seek a better and unified world. A better understanding among nations might be the result of the quests mentioned above, which could result in more cultural similarities among both groups in terms of shared values and lifestyles. This is a daring and quite optimistic proposition; however, it does not seem impossible.

4.6 Literature review: conclusions and research gap

The literature review revealed the importance of destination image in attracting tourists. It also demonstrated the influence of socio-demographic factors on the image formation process and that an image may vary among individuals and countries. The latter proposition appeared to be controversial with some sources claiming the presence of global tourists, allowing consideration of the world market as homogenous. It is purported that youths particularly portray what is seen as the global tourist due to their propensity for influence by globalisation.

Nevertheless, the analysis on globalisation and its effects on consumer behaviour illustrated reverse effects. Some cultures appear to defend themselves from globalisation in an attempt to demonstrate the non-acceptance of different values and lifestyles, which also impinges on their consumer behaviour. However, also in this context, youths, but especially youths from the Arab world, seem to be more open-minded and accepting of globalisation (Figure 4.3). The detailed analysis of Arab and Protestant youth cultures demonstrated that Arabs are about to absorb more features of Western culture. On the other hand, Protestant European youth are striving for a more unified and better world. This may result in finding some common ground on which to base an improved coexistence in the future by sharing similar thoughts, ideals etc, facilitated by improved communication tools, such as the internet. Thus, the question of whether youths from two cultural backgrounds show similarities to an extent that they can be considered as a homogenous market appears reasonable. For a tourist destination such as Berlin, a more homogenous market would mean that marketing expenditures could be cut, since different markets require different marketing strategies at present, according to Gruber (2008), Assistant Manager at BTM. For example, if Arabs and Protestant Europeans have similar images of Berlin, they could both be promoted with the same marketing tools.

Figure 4.3: Is globalisation causing homogeneity in consumer behaviour?

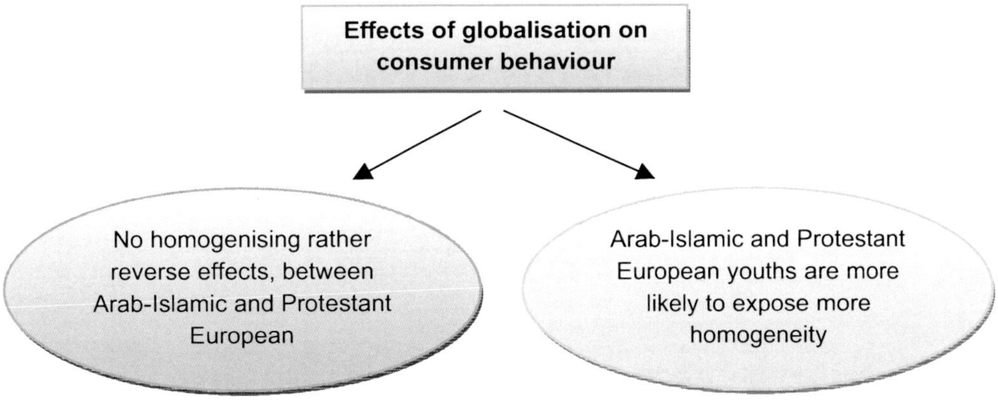

Berlin's general image among tourists, mainly from the Western world, is positive but how Berlin is perceived as a tourist destination in the Arab world remains unanswered. Cross-cultural image studies on Berlin's destination image seem to be entirely missing. Overall, little is known about the Arab tourist. As Finucane (2008) illustrates, only a small number of academics *'in the Western world, know anything of* Arabs' and their way of life since they are scarcely examined in tourism studies. Consequently, no sources could be located in which the Arab and the traditional Protestant tourist have been compared. Therefore, cross-cultural studies are required, especially in terms of destination image.

Hence, the author decided to conduct primary research to discover similarities and differences in the perception of Berlin among youths from Protestant Europe and the Arab world (Middle East). The following chapter explains the author's approach to primary research.

Chapter Five: Methodology

5.1   Introduction

In order to answer the research question, the author has used secondary sources. The first four research objectives could be reached by literature study; however, secondary sources could not fulfil the following objective:

> ➢ Are there cross-cultural differences in the perception of Berlin as a tourist destination among youth tourists from traditionally Protestant countries and Arab youth tourists?

Consequently, primary research was necessary to fill the knowledge gap. This chapter will explain how primary data was collected, justifying the methods used as well as their validity and reliability.

5.2   Research philosophy

Research method literatures mention a wide range of different research approaches, dimensions and issues. According to Gliner and Morgan (2000, p.10) the following research dimensions are vital:

> ➢   Theoretical versus applied
> ➢   Inductive versus deductive
> ➢   Positivism versus Interpretivism versus Realism
> ➢   Quantitative versus qualitative research

Although various dimensions are confronted in this case, it does not mean that a research project cannot adapt more than one dimension (Gliner and Morgan 2000, p.11). A complex study can simultaneously apply quantitative and qualitative research, for instance. The objective of this sub chapter is to reflect on the different philosophical research approaches adopted by this study.

5.2.1   Applied research

The OECD (2001) defines applied research as an *'original investigation undertaken in order to acquire new knowledge. It is, however, directed primarily towards a specific practical aim or objective'.* Unlike theoretical research, applied research is not as universal in its scope and applies existing theoretical knowledge to particular problems in order to solve them rather than generate totally new knowledge (Veal 2006, p.33). The aim of the applied scientist is more to enhance *'the human condition'* (Gilner and Morgan 2000, p.18). Applied research is additionally considered as having commercial objectives and often arises in policy, planning and management situations where an abundant number of theories already exists and theories are applied to unravel problems (Veal 2006, p.33). Therefore, applied research seems to be most applicable to this study.

5.2.2   Deductive research

Research generally combines finding out and explaining certain phenomena (Veal 2006, p.34). Veal (2006, p.34) suggests that finding out incorporates describing and gathering information, while explaining means to comprehend that information. Deductive research resembles scientific research the most, as it involves the testing of theory (Saunders *et al.* 2003, p.86). In order to visualise the general research process, Veal developed a circular model (Figure 5.1). Within the circular model, a deductive approach commences by forming a hypothesis [c], which is subsequently tested by conducting further research [a] and eventually the outcome is analysed [b].

Figure 5.1: Circular model of research approaches

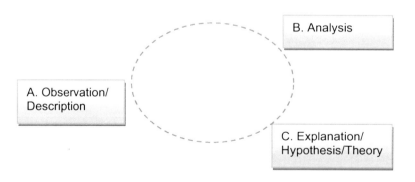

Source: Veal 2006, p.34

Deductive reasoning intends to test a research question or theory and requires logical analysis and interpretation to accomplish an expressive result (Veal 1997, p.30). The sequential stages of deductive research concur with the approach of this research project.

5.2.3   Positivism, interpretivism and realism

Three types of philosophies dictate the research process; positivsm, interpretivism and realism (Saunders *et al.* 2003, p.83).

The framework of the positivist's research incorporates that human beings and their actions can be studied from the outside and that the findings are explained on the basis of facts by the researcher, *'using theories and models developed by researchers'* (Fisher 2004, p.15, Saunders *et al.* 2003, p.83, Veal 2006, p.37). The positivist claims that tangible aspects of human life, such as behaviour and speech, are scientifically measurable (Fisher 2004, p.15). However, owing to his stance, he ignores the internal motivations and causes of behaviour, which are not measurable according to him (Saunders *et al.* 2003, p.83). In this respect, the positivist's view does not correspond to this study's nature, given that the destination image formation process is also influenced by an individual's internal factors, which the positivist would disregard (Beerli & Martin 2004, Di Marino 2008). The positivist's aim is to generate law-like generalisations, as a result of the research process (Fisher 2004, p.15, Remenyi *et al.* 1998 cited Saunders *et al.* 2003, p.83), which is not the aim of this study.

At this point, the interpretivist's perspective coincides more with the aim of this study. Today's business world is fast changing and too complex to be theorised by definite laws (Saunders *et al.* 2003, p.84). Each business situation is a fundamentally unique matter. Each situation displays varying characteristics and needs to be interpreted individually, so generalising cannot be perceived as being efficient. The interpretive model additionally relies on the studied objects to provide their own subjective explanations of their situation and actions, which enable the researcher to see the world from their perspective (Saunders *et al.* 2003, p.84, Veal 2006, p.37) Especially in cross-cultural study, the interpretivist view seems appropriate, because he or she realises that individuals are influenced by their environment and social construct and may therefore place different interpretations on the same matter (Saunders *et al.* 2003, p.84).

The realist holds numerous ambitions of positivism, yet he considers the subjective nature of research (Fisher 2004, p.15). He or she suggests the necessity to comprehend *'people's socially constructed interpretations'*, in order to recognise broader external and internal factors that influence people's views and behaviours (Saunders *et al.* 2003, p.85). Furthermore, they are aware that the world is too complex to understand every aspect of life and believe that researchers need to accept their findings cannot be generalised, because different researchers with different values will develop competing theories (Fisher 2004, p.16).

Consequently, this study also takes a realist approach on the basis of acknowledging that it can only give explanations and indications to the phenomena of destination image and its culture-specificity. The scope of this study is too small to establish new ideas in the topic of cross-culturally perceived destination image. Hence, this research adopts a combination of the positivist's and the interpretivist's view with the stance of a realist.

5.3   Primary research

Primary research was required to fulfil the objective mentioned in the introduction. Veal (1997, p.33) states that primary research is necessary where existing data cannot achieve the study's aim. In this context, the researcher's subject is under-researched and hence necessitates further investigation.

Consequently a questionnaire (Appendix 6) was created in three different languages namely English, German and Arabic. The English questionnaire was published on surveymonkey.com, which provided the researcher with an individual link to his survey. This link was randomly sent via e-mail to several hundred Arab-Islamic and Protestant European youth who were asked to fill in the questionnaire. Online surveys have the advantage, that the answers are minimally distorted due to the anonymity of such methods (Saunders *et al.* 2003, p.284). Several other sources were also applied to reach potential interviewees:

> *Social networks*, such as facebook.com, xing.com, studivz.de and wordpress.com

- ➢ *Forums* on the German-Arabic youth-website 'Li-Lak' of the Goethe Institute
- ➢ *Mailings* were sent to students at Bournemouth University and NHTV Breda.

The Arabic copy of the questionnaire was distributed by the author's father in Abu Dhabi (UAE), where 48 copies were completed. Furthermore, the author conducted 21 structured face-to-face interviews in Bournemouth, where a lot of Arab students are located, owing to the large number of language schools in Bournemouth.

Altogether, the researcher collected 367 responses in 28 days (10/07/2008 – 08/08/2008). However, not all respondents matched the study's target group from a socio-demographic point of view, so it was necessary to filter the responses. Survey participants had to meet the following criteria to be considered for the study:

- ➢ Protestant-European or Arab-Isamic background
- ➢ Aged between 15 and 25
- ➢ No previous visit to Berlin.

Eventually, 239 respondents met the criteria. In total, 103 Arab youths responded along with 136 youths from traditionally Protestant countries. Both groups had to fill in the same questionnaire, which allowed the researcher to undertake inner-cultural interpretations of the findings prior to conducting cross-cultural comparisons. Kozak *et al.* (2003) stress the importance to use the same measures across cultures in order to accomplish meaningful results.

However, Choi *et al.* (2007) suggest applying multivariate research methods to identify destination image constructs. Qualitative research was also carried out because it is increasingly acknowledged as a valuable complement to quantitative research where the recognition of destination image is concerned. Several semi-structured in-depth interviews (see 6.2.3) were carried out at EF School in Bournemouth based on the questionnaire. EF school allowed the researcher to undertake primary research in three different classes, in which students from various countries (including Protestant European and Arab-Islamic) were interviewed in groups. The interviews lasted approximately 20 minutes and were recorded.

A few students appeared to be introvert and did not sufficiently contribute to the interview session; hence, at the end of the interviews, all students were asked to express their feelings towards Berlin by writing two or three sentences on a sheet of paper (Appendix 7). They were also asked to add their nationality, age and gender, so that the researcher was able to allocate the statements at a later point.

Furthermore, when the survey link was forwarded to several hundred youth, they were asked to send back an e-mail which expressed their mental picture of Berlin. Although the response rate was low – 9 of which 7 could be used for the analysis – these responses were valuable for the analytical process.

5.4   Quantitative and qualitative data analysis

This study applied quantitative and qualitative data collection methods. Many researchers associate qualitative research with an inductive approach, and quantitative research with a deductive approach. However, Long (2007, p.193) claims there is no logical reason why the approaches should not be employed in both directions.

Questionnaire surveys usually require quantitative methods (Veal 1997, p.146), which may be more reliable as they underlie *'universal rules and standardised procedures'* (Berkowitz 1997, Blaxter *et al.* 2001, p.65). Furthermore, numerical data facilitates the process of analysing data and appears to have more expressiveness. Veal (1997, p.146) states that quantitative methods are more applicable where *'attitudes, meanings and perceptions among the population as a whole'* are being investigated.

Kelly (1980 cited Veal 2006, p.195) objects to the latter supposition by arguing that qualitative procedures are more reliable in understanding people's needs and aspirations. Questionnaire surveys tend to shape respondents answers, which consequently limit the analysis (Vitale *et al.* 2008). Hence, a qualitative approach was conducted to capture people's psychological and holistic impressions connected to Berlin, which are difficult to collect by quantitative methods (Choi *et al.* 2007).

5.5   Survey sample

As mentioned in 5.3, the researcher collected 376 responses in total of which 239 were relevant. According to Kozak *et al.* (2003), the sample of any cross-cultural study needs to be homogenous concerning their socio-demographic characteristics and, only if such characteristics are similar, is data comparable. In other words, it would be meaningless to compare third agers with youths.

Therefore, probability sampling was used to reach as many people as possible from the respective focus group and a stratified random sampling procedure was considered to be most suitable. Saunders *et al.* (2003, p.490) define the latter procedure as a *'probability sampling procedure in which the population is divided into two or more relevant strata and a random sample (systematic or simple) is drawn from each of the strata'*. The researcher divided the population by targeting youths from two cultural backgrounds. Subsequently, he identified online forums and online social networks, where the probability to reach the focus group was high. The hyperlink for the questionnaire was randomly forwarded to these forums and social networks so the possibility of people outside the focus group responding to the questionnaire was minimised, but not ruled out. Accordingly, respondents not matching the socio-demographic requirements were filtered out from the study.

In consideration of the study's qualitative research, the researcher selected groups of people that were relevant to the study. Long (2007, p.42) calls this approach theoretical sampling. However, EF School Bournemouth could not arrange classes in which only Arab-Islamic and Protestant Europeans were included, which meant that the interviewed groups also included students from Asia, from other parts of Europe or students that were older than 25. They were also involved in the interviews for ethical reasons, but their contributions were excluded from the analysis.

Despite the researcher's willingness to provide a representative and relevant study, it needs to be noted that the sample cannot be regarded as representative for the respective populations due to the constrained sample size, so the sample is supposedly biased.

5.6 Questionnaire design

The questionnaire was divided into two parts:

> ➢ Finding out the tourists' profiles (Question 1a to e & 2)
> ➢ Questions about Berlin's Image as a tourist destination (Q 3 to 8)

The first and the second question were posed to ensure that all respondents met the criteria, mentioned in 5.3, to be included in this study

A rising number of destination image studies incorporate Echtner and Brent-Ritchie's three-dimensional continuum of destination image for the measurement of image (Di Marino 2007). Thus, the formulation of the questionnaire was based on Echtner and Brent-Ritchie's diagram (2003) of the four components of destination image (Figure 5.2). For each of the components - psychological attributes, functional attributes, functional holistic and psychological holistic – a question was formulated and a list of attributes compiled that intended to identify individuals' perception of Berlin regarding each component. For example, under psychological attributes, nine destination attributes were listed in order to find out people's image of Berlin in this respect.

Figure 5.2: The four components of destination image

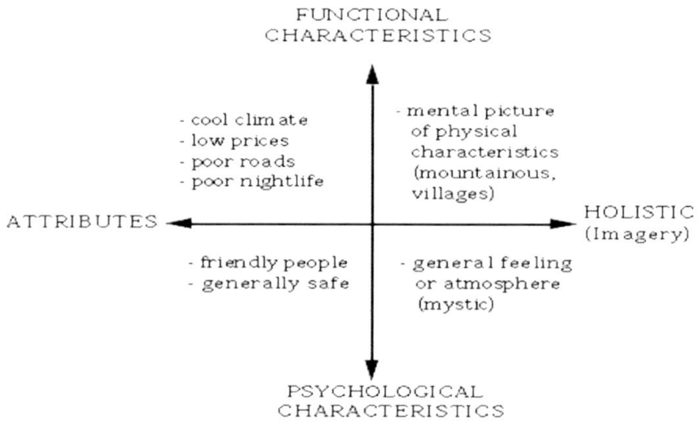

Source: The Journal of Tourism Studies 2003. 14 (1), p. 43

Afterwards, mean values were calculated for each of the four dimensions, which enabled the researcher to create a perceptual map on a coordinate system that enabled the illustration of cross-cultural divergences regarding the image after the analysis.

The questionnaire employed rating questions in order to gather opinion data. A five-point Likert-style rating scale was used. Various destination attributes were then listed under each of the dimensions listed above and the interviewees could state their level of agreement from strongly agree to strongly disagree. Albaum (1997) purports that Likert scales are particularly valuable where people's attitude towards objects is examined and was thus regarded as most suitable for this study.

The semi-structured group interviews were also conducted on the basis of the original questionnaire; however, open-ended questions were used in this case.

5.7   Pilot questionnaire

The questionnaire was pilot tested in order to identify potential weaknesses (Appendix 8). Pilot tests help *'to refine the questionnaire'*, as well as receive some evaluation of the questions' *'validity and the likely reliability'* of the eventual collected data (Saunders *et al.* 2007, p.386).

The questionnaire was pilot tested by distributing ten copies randomly among friends and relatives. The researcher watched the interviewees while they were filling in the questionnaire and was able to identify certain weaknesses.

Firstly, the questionnaire additionally needed a preface in order to introduce respondents to the topic. The pilot questionnaires revealed that people thought that they had to be familiar with Berlin in order to participate. Consequently, the introduction had to clarify that the questionnaire intended to identify people's mental picture of Berlin, which did not require extensive knowledge about the destination.

Furthermore, question 7 had to be reworded, since the original question seemed to be confusing and misleading. For question 3, the researcher had to underline that only one answer could be ticked, so a remark was added accordingly.

5.8   Data analysis

Following completion of the survey, obtained data was entered into SPSS. Frequencies and means were calculated for each variable and several ANOVA tests (explained in Appendix 9) and cross-tabulations conducted in order to stress destination image's specificity in terms of cultural background.

5.9   Research limitations

The researcher's intention to make this study as relevant as possible and to ascertain its validity and reliability played an important role. However, the nature of the research and its approach involves limitations.

Validity is based on collected information that *'truly reflects the phenomenon being studied'* (Veal 1997, p. 35). Contrary to natural science studies, tourism based research underlies a variety of *'imperfections'* in its approach (Veal 1997, p.35). Empirical research, which originates out of conclusions on data collected, discloses a major weakness because it relies on the population's responses to questionnaires, for instance (Veal 1997, p.35). Consequently, the analysis of such a questionnaire merely reveals an approximation rather than actual facts on people's behavioural trends.

According to Veal (1997, p.35), *'reliability is the extent to which research findings would be the same if the research was to be repeated at a later date'.* In order to establish the outcome of the research, it would be necessary to replicate the study a subsequently so that a comparison could demonstrate any fluctuations in responses. Hence, the reliability of the research outcome cannot be guaranteed since the author's time constraints prevent him from repeating the research project. The study also presents a *'snap-shot picture of a group of people',* which is subject to modification over time (Veal 1997, p.36).

Furthermore, the likert scales used for the questionnaire have certain weaknesses in cross-cultural studies because the interpretation of the strength of a scale may vary from one tourist to another (de Moiji 2004, p.309, Pareek and Rao 1980 cited Kozak *et al.* 2003). While the neutral scale could mean 'no opinion' to one group, it could mean 'mild agreement' to another; therefore, some results may be distorted. Kozak *et al.* (2003) add that *'it is easier to record cross-cultural differences than it is to prove that this is because of cultural differences'*. In order to minimise any distortion of the results, semi-structured face-to-face interviews were carried out because they probe more deeply into an individual's attitude towards an object (Veal 2006, p.197).

5.10   Summary

The methodological framework of this study has been outlined in this chapter, which demonstrated that primary research was central for this study to answer the last objective. Primary research was undertaken through quantitative and qualitative data collection methods. Quantitative methods incorporated the distribution of the questionnaire via the Internet and on-street, whereas qualitative methods involved several interviews with focus groups. Altogether, these research methods were effective in collecting an expressive number of respondents and interviewees. An overview is provided in table 5.1. The following chapter unveils the primary research findings and analyses the data.

Table 5.1: An overview of this study's research methods

1.Research philosophy	➤ **Combination of positivist's, interpretivist's view and realist's stance**
2. Primary research	➤ Questionnaire published on surveymonkey.com ○ Hyperlink sent to various social networks ➤ Field research in Abu Dhabi and Bournemouth ➤ Semi-structured interviews with focus groups at EF School Bournemouth ➤ In total 239 relevant responses collected
3. Sampling	➤ Probability sampling → Stratified random
4. Questionnaire design	➤ Formulation of questions based on Echtner and Brent Ritchie's (2003) model of 'The four components of destination image'
5. Data analysis	➤ SPSS → One-Way ANOVA tests and Cross tabulations in particular

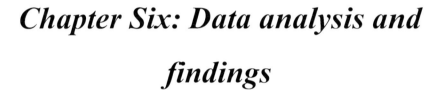

Chapter Six: Data analysis and findings

6.1 Introduction

This chapter presents the findings from the questionnaires and interviews and focuses on identifying cultural differences or similarities in the perception of Berlin among Arab-Islamic and Protestant European youths. Other influencing factors of destination image such as age, gender etc are not considered. Collected quantitative data was analysed with the aid of SPSS software. The implementation of SPSS allowed the author to carry out cross-tabulations and ANOVA tests to determine the effect of culture on the perception of Berlin as a tourist destination. The significance level for the ANOVA was set at 95%, which determines the amount of divergences required to establish significant differences between the cultural groups. In Appendices10 to 16, a detailed list of SPSS outcomes can be consulted.

6.2 Respondents' profile

239 people participated in the survey. 86% of them were 19 to 25 years and 14% 15 to 18 years old. Due to the low number of respondents aged 15 to 18 years, the factor age was not analysed in relation to destination image, as the results would not have been meaningful. Most participants were female (57%). Besides, none of the surveyees, that are considered in the analysis, has ever been to Berlin.

6.2.1 Demographic characteristics: Protestant European survey participants

57% of all respondents had a Protestant-European background. As figure 6.1 visualises, most of them originated from the Netherlands (38%) followed by the UK (18%), Germany (15%), Norway (12%), Denmark (11%) and Sweden (9%).

Figure 6.1: Country of origin

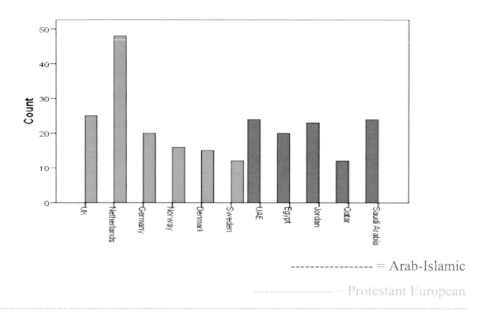

A significant female bias could be noted within the group with only 32% being male respondents (Figure 6.2). Besides, most respondents were quite educated with 46% having completed an undergraduate University course and 13% having a Master or PhD (Figure 6.3). 19% stated they are at University or at least have been there, whereas 21% finished their education at a high school or a lower level.

6.2.2 Demographic characteristics: Arab-Islamic survey participants

43% of all respondents had an Arab-Islamic background. The majority of these respondents came from the UAE and Saudi Arabia (23%) followed by Jordan (22%), Egypt (19%) and Qatar (12%).

Figure 6.2: Cultural background and gender

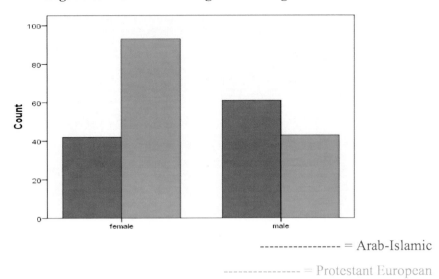

----------------- = Arab-Islamic

---------------- = Protestant European

Initially a strong male bias was expected among Arab-Islamic participants but that did not occur with 59% being male and 41% being female. However, the small male bias among Arabs is offset with the strong female bias among Protestant Europeans and may distort the findings of this study, as destination image is assumed to be gender-specific (Beerli and Martin 2004).

Figure 6.3: Cultural background and education

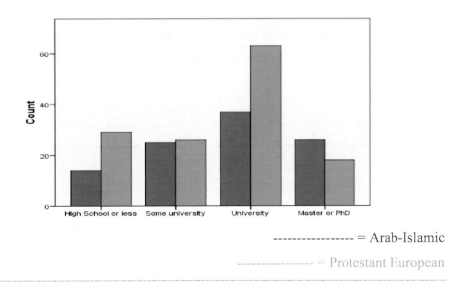

----------------- = Arab-Islamic

---------------- = Protestant European

Similar to Protestant-European participants, Arab-Islamic ones were also quite cultivated. 25% claimed to have a Master or PhD degree, 36% an undergraduate degree, 25% to have attended University and 14% finished at High School or at a lower level.

In order to conduct expressive cross-cultural studies, it is vital to compare groups that share similar lifestyles and are as homogenous as possible. This study has achieved that.

6.2.3 Demographic characteristics of focus group interviewees and other qualitative data collection methods

The focus group interviews were conducted in three different classes at EF School in Bournemouth. The first and second interviews were carried out with a whole class of students from varying backgrounds. Some students did not meet this study's socio-demographic requirements, so they were excluded from the analysis and marked in red within figure 6.4. In a different class, the author received the teacher's permission to undertake more individual interviews with smaller groups (3rd to 5th Interviews). In total, four Arab-Islamic students were interviewed and eleven Protestant-Europeans.

Figure 6.4: Focus group interviews at EF School, Bournemouth

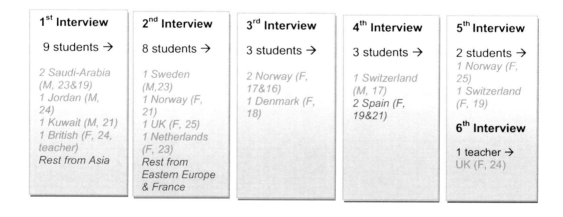

The author also received eight written comments about Berlin via e-mail (Appendix 7). Two of the respondents were from Jordan (F, 24 & M, 24), two from Egypt (F, 21 & 23), the Netherlands (M, 25), Switzerland (F, 19) and two from Denmark (F, 18 & 25). A strong female-bias also emerged through the profile of focus group interviewees.

6.3   What comes first to your mind, when you think about Berlin?

This question was asked because people's initial thoughts about a place may affect their general attitude towards it and be responsible for the formation of the final image.

The first thing that came into participants' minds when thinking of Berlin was history (44%) and capital (24%). Within their groups, most Arab-Islamic and Protestant-European respondents (44%) mentioned history as Berlin's most prevailing feature followed by capital (22% & 25%).

In this context, an ANOVA test was conducted (Table 6.1) in order to identify a potential correlation of cultural background and first impression of Berlin. However, statistical data did not reveal significant cross-cultural differences, as highlighted in the table.

Table 6.1: One-way ANOVA test on 'what comes first into your mind when you think of Berlin?

Between groups	Sum of Squares	F	Sig.
	4.806	.762	.383

However, qualitative data was more meaningful. In connection with history, the 'Brandenburger Tor' and particularly the Berlin Wall were often mentioned. A few Arab and British interviewees related Berlin primarily with the War, which may bring about negative impressions and affect one's image.

'The big swastika from the war hanging in the square, it is not negative, just historical'.

-Female, UK, 25-

'Cold war, the Berlin Wall and history'

-Male, Saudi-Arabia, 23-

Both interviewees firstly referred to the Second World War and its implications, which demonstrate the degree to which Berlin's image is yet widely affected by the appalling events of 60 years ago. Nevertheless, other Protestants considered Berlin's history more as positive and exciting.

'Many different things, history, different buildings, Brandenburger Tor, it's very much different, many different buildings'

-Female, Norway, 17-

Protestant Europeans, except for Britons, seemed to affiliate Berlin's history with excitement and did not directly refer to the War, as Arabs and Britons did in the first instance. This might indicate that Scandinavians are inclined to be more positive concerning Berlin than other Protestant Europeans, which will be further scrutinised throughout this chapter. Consequently, this might already suggest inner-cultural as well as cross-cultural divergences in the perception of Berlin.

6.4   Question 4: Functional attributes of Berlin & the level of agreement

The list of statements under the fourth question in the survey intended to capture participants' image of individual functional attributes regarding Berlin. On the whole, the mean values of the ANOVA demonstrated that the majority of respondents commonly rated the functional attributes highly. Arab-Islamic and Protestant-European respondents showed comparable tendencies in their responses by mainly agreeing with functional attributes, such as 'rich cultural offer', 'interesting historical sites' and 'good infrastructure'. The lowest evaluations were given to fair prices and rich gastronomy by Arabs, while Protestants concurred least with various parks/nature and fair prices.

Table 6.2: One-way ANOVA test on functional attributes by cultural background

Between groups	Sum of Squares	F	Sig.
Fair prices	7.878	11.437	.001
Good infrastructure	.478	.478	.321
Easy accessibility	9.191	18.072	.000
Rich gastronomy	8.514	9.035	.003
Good quality of accommodation	.074	.140	.709
Good shopping	.044	.071	.790
Rich cultural offer	.146	.237	.627
Brilliant nightlife	3.536	4.502	.035
Interesting historical sights	4.290	8.717	.003
Various parks/nature	6.011	7.428	.007

Subsequently, an ANOVA was conducted which recognised significant differences between the groups in six of ten (60%) functional attributes, highlighted in table 6.2. Strikingly, Arabs evaluated various parks/nature higher and seemed to perceive Berlin as green, which became salient throughout the collection of primary data. Nevertheless, it also appeared that Arabs did not particularly think of Berlin as being green, but rather of Europe, thereupon places within Europe had to be green according to them.

> *'I think it's green city because it is in Europe...we have an image of Europe being not like our countries...and very good infrastructure because it is in Europe'*
>
> -Male, 23, Saudi Arabia-

Most Arabs made similar statements. As a consequence, Arabs blatantly did not distinguish between Berlin and Europe or Germany, since they did not seem to have a distinct notion of the city. Berlin did not stimulate clear images among Arabs, which also emerged during the implementation of group discussions. As an example, when Arabs were asked to name some unique cultural attractions, the response rate was low in the first instance and, if a statement was made, it was merely related to the Second World War.

'War, tanks and the wall'

-Male, 19, Saudi Arabia-

'Architecture like from the Second World War very strong'

-Male, 24, Jordan-

Periodically, respondents from Protestant Europe had a blurred picture too; however, they tended to give more responses and to name more features that coincided with contemporary Berlin.

'A lot of Turkish people...because of the World War a lot of building sites, still not noisy, but rather organised. A lot of parks...'

-Male, 23, Sweden-

'Many different things, history, different buildings, Brandenburger Tor, it's very much different, many different buildings'

-Female, 17, Norway-

'Berlin is completely modern now with a thriving nightlife, cultural life, cuisine. Very popular with tourists....possibly very expensive'

-Female, 23, UK-

During the interviews, some Protestant Europeans mentioned Berlin's brilliant nightlife, when they spoke of Berlin.

'Nightlife and entertainment comes to my mind first'

-Female, 24, UK-

Arabs, on the other hand, associated Berlin to a much lesser extent with 'brilliant nightlife', as proved by the quantitative data as well as the qualitative data. Arabs appeared to have a fixed image of serious and cold Germans, so, from their perspective; any fun-related attributes would apparently not match their picture of Berlin.

In terms of evaluating the functional attribute 'fair prices', the ANOVA test revealed significant differences between the groups. At this point, Arabs agreed less than their counterparts. Semi-structured interviews were indicative of the potential reason for the differences. While many Protestant Europeans might know that Berlin is one of the cheapest capitals in Europe (Stengel 2005), Arabs affiliated the place with luxury products, such as health tourism or Mercedes. The latter once more shows that Arabs did not distinguish between Berlin and Germany either, since Mercedes originally comes from Stuttgart.

'I think Germany in health-care tourism is famous in Kuwait...'

-Male, 21, Kuwait-

'All Saudis go to Germany for medical tourism and to buy Mercedes'

-Male, 23, Saudi Arabia-

The ANOVA test further demonstrated relevant differences between the groups regarding the assessment of 'interesting historical sights'; qualitative data confirmed this. Even though Arabs also referred to Berlin's considerable past, it was not to the extent that Protestant Europeans did. They seemed to know that Berlin possesses a remarkable past but, in terms of interesting related sights, only a small number mentioned the Berlin Wall, for instance. Protestant Europeans knew more about Berlin and its sights of historical interest.

'When I try to visualise Berlin, I can see a remarkable combination of the old and the modern. Sadly, I can't give any examples: the Berlin Wall is the only thing that springs to mind'

-Male, 24, Jordan-

'It is full of history...lots of young people drinking beer around Brandenburg Door and...tourists buying pieces of the Berlin Wall and...to see...of the Holocaust'

-Female, 18, Denmark-

In addition to overall differences between Arabs and Protestants, small inner-cultural differences could be found among Protestant Europeans from the Nordic countries (Sweden, Norway and Denmark) and from the UK, the Netherlands and Germany. Respondents from Nordic countries were quite homogenous in their responses, as the mean values in table 6.3 illustrate (1 = strongly agree & 5 strongly disagree). In aggregate, they assessed Berlin higher, not particularly in terms of individual functional attributes, but throughout the analysis, Scandinavians tended to be more positive regarding Berlin. Inner-cultural differences among Arab participants could not be noted in this instance.

Table 6.3: Average means of responses under functional attributes by nationality

UK = 2.0	Netherlands = 2.2	Germany = 1.9
Norway = 2.1	Denmark = 2.0	Sweden = 2.1

Eventually, qualitative and quantitative data signified relevant cultural differences between the groups as a whole, so it can be concluded that cultural background affected the evaluation of Berlin's functional destination attributes.

6.5 Question 5: Psychological attributes of Berlin & the level of agreement

The fifth question of the survey attempted to capture participants' evaluation of Berlin concerning psychological attributes. In aggregate, most respondents concurred with the attributes 'fun/enjoyable' and 'clean'. Remarkably, the attributes 'friendly people' and 'young' were, by far, the least endorsed, albeit Berlin is actually a young city. Once again, this point shows that the participants' image of Berlin might have been distorted, as mentioned in 6.4.

Table 6.4: One-way ANOVA test on psychological attributes by cultural background

Between groups	Sum of Squares	F	Sig.
Friendly people	13.340	15.016	.000
Generally safe	2.120	3.547	.061
Clean	21.999	27.219	.000
Young	.064	.092	.762
Fun/enjoyable	.807	1.397	.238

In order to find out a possible correlation between cultural background and perception of Berlin's psychological attributes, an ANOVA test was conducted. Table 6.4 denotes the results and highlights the significant differences. In just two of five (40%) psychological attributes, significant differences were categorised between Arab-Islamic and Protestant Europeans, which contests destination image's culture-specificity in this regard.

Significant differences occurred in the evaluation of Berlin's cleanliness which Arabs assessed notably higher than Protestant Europeans. In turn, the latter group assessed 'friendly people' higher, yet, overall, the attribute 'friendly people' received one of the lowest evaluations. The interviews revealed that people from Berlin were saliently affiliated with rather negative features, especially by Arab and partly by British participants.

'I have a lot of German friends and quite a lot of them are from Berlin...from the point of view of a British person, I find them quite narrow-minded...I would be quite interested to know...what it is like for an immigrant in Berlin. I would think it'd be a little bit difficult. And consequently, it must be difficult for a tourist to be there'

-Female, 24, UK-

'Unfriendly, cause...I have this impression, but I am not sure'

-Male, 23, Saudi Arabia-

*'I think they are a bit arrogant...the houses are very well organised, the
gardens of people very well tidied'*

-Male, 19, Saudi Arabia-

Strikingly, people from Berlin were frequently labelled in correspondence with the German stereotype that is often regarded as serious, organised, strict and narrow-minded. Stereotyping might also be the reason why Arabs considered Berlin more often as clean than did Protestant Europeans, since Germans are perceived as clean.

On the contrary, Scandinavians, as well as Dutch people, tended to be more positive in respect of people in Berlin and the psychological attributes in general (Table 6.5). Additionally, when a group of Scandinavian girls were asked to describe a person from Berlin, they were apt to be more affirmative.

*'Very cool and trendy, very self-confident, cheek, a little bit charming but not
very, nice and friendly'*

-Female, 16, Norway-

'It's funny and people are very nice'

-Female, 17, Norway-

'I consider Berliners to be quite easy-going and funny'

-Male, 25, Netherlands-

Like previous findings, this proves that Scandinavians were more positive towards Berlin than other Protestant Europeans were (Table 6.6) and, simultaneously, more homogenous as a sub-group of historically Protestant countries. Arab-Islamic participants again appeared to rate Berlin more in consideration of Germany as a whole, rather than in exact contemplation of Berlin as an individual place. German stereotypes appear to dominate their image of Berlin. Among Arabs though, no significant inner-cultural differences were discovered.

Table 6.5: Average means of responses under psychological attributes by nationality

UK = 2.6	Netherlands = 2.5	Germany = 2.6
Norway = 2.3	Denmark = 2.3	Sweden = 2.3

Statistical data revealed cross-cultural differences in only 40% of the listed psychological attributes, which does not clarify whether destination image is culture-specific in respect of these attributes. Yet, qualitative data proved that people's attitudes towards Berlin varied cross-culturally. Arabs were more negative by mainly imagining unfriendly people in Berlin, while Scandinavians and Dutch had a contrary image. Strikingly, the British perspective resembled the Arabs' perspective, which might still be an effect of the Second World War, in which Germany and the UK were enemies. Matussek (cited Smee 2006) adds that Britons love clinging to Second World War clichés and simply do not like Germany. The World War seems to affect Britons' image of Berlin, which will become clearer in the process of this chapter.

'...the coverage of television in the history after World War 2, we get a lot of that on British TV'

-Female, 24, UK-

Consequently, a correlation between cultural background and the perception of psychological attributes regarding Berlin could be established. However, Britons' evaluation of certain psychological attributes resembled more the evaluation of Arabs, which may indicate inner-cultural differences too.

6.6   Question 6: Functional holistic picture of Berlin

The sixth question in the survey attempted to capture participants' mental picture of Berlin. Most respondents agreed that Berlin was 'modern', 'multi-cultural' and had a 'vivid cityscape', while Berlin was lesser regarded as 'noble/classy', 'green' and 'tolerant'.

Concerning the respondents' mental picture of Berlin, an ANOVA was carried out (Table 6.6) and acknowledged relevant cross-cultural differences in four of eight factors (50%). The Arab–Islamic and Protestant European groups showed significant differences in the evaluation of Berlin in terms of the attributes 'multi-cultural', 'modern', 'vivid cityscape' and 'green'. Noticeably, the groups also demonstrated considerable divergences in the perception of Berlin regarding the factors 'well-groomed' (91%), 'noble' (94.8%), 'beautiful' (84%) and 'tolerant' (77%). The percentages in brackets illustrate the extent to which differences are true in statistical terms, albeit they are still not statistically significant. However, it emerges overall that people's mental picture of Berlin was not homogenous across cultures.

Table 6.6: One-way ANOVA test on the functional holistic picture by cultural background

Between groups	Sum of Squares	F	Sig.
Vivid cityscape	16.115	21.502	.000
Green	15.930	16.571	.000
Multi-cultural	5.301	6.088	.014
Well-groomed	1.450	2.893	.090
Noble/classy	2.818	3.818	.052
Beautiful	1.619	1.992	.159
Tolerant	1.035	1.472	.226
Modern	9.375	16.453	.000

Qualitative data could further establish cultural differences in people's mental picture of Berlin. For example, regarding the factor 'multi-cultural', both groups considered Berlin to be cosmopolitan. The comments of Arab participants often had a negative touch attached to them and questioned people's tolerance in Berlin, while Protestant Europeans judged this aspect more positively.

'I heard from friends that many foreigners in Berlin, but also strong racial segregation…which is a consequence from the war'

-Female, 24, Jordan-

'Berlin is a cosmopolitan city, adapted to new ways of life...'

-Female, 18, Denmark-

This negative touch from the Arab's perspective also occurred in further responses regarding the expected atmosphere in Berlin. Arabs seemed to think that the atmosphere in Berlin would be cold, whereas Protestant Europeans associated it rather with excitement.

'Berlin is a cold...city'

-Male, 24, Jordan-

'Berlin a big city, high buildings and cold. Not really sunny with serious and organised people'

-Male, 23, Saudi Arabia-

'...very busy, yeah busy, I think full of life you know...very exciting'

-Female, 17, Norway-

'Compared to other German places, Berlin must be very active and lively...'

-Female, 25, Denmark-

Furthermore, Arabs blatantly perceived Berlin more as 'green', which the ANOVA and the analysis in 6.4 revealed. In general, it appeared that Arab respondents perceived Berlin negatively in regard of affective components of destination image, while, in regard of cognitive components, they are rather neutral to positive. In fact, Arabs seem to be negative when Berlin's attributes are closely linked to its people (e.g. tolerant, multi-cultural & friendly people), which may be a consequence of an overall bad image of Germans. Germans were often perceived as unfriendly, uncooperative and narrow-minded.

'If you go to Switzerland, Spain they would like to speak with you in English. I'm not sure if I'm right or not but in Germany they don't like to speak'

-Male, 23, Saudi Arabia-

Alternatively, Arabs are more affirmative in the evaluation of objects or cognitive components (e.g. modern, beautiful and well-groomed) in relation to Germany. The following statements support this proposition.

'Berlin must be really beautiful in the summer, very green and organised'

-Female, 23, Egypt-

Protestant Europeans do not share the same stance towards Berlin and its people and consider them as open-minded.

'Berlin is an open-minded and cosmopolitan city...'

-Male, 25, Netherlands-

On the other hand, in the evaluation of cognitive components, they are more reserved and constantly rated Berlin lower than the Arabs did. Protestant Europeans might simply not associate Berlin with particularly modern, because they might experience similar standards in their home-countries, so this aspect does not predominantly come into their mind when thinking of Berlin. Arabs though may not be used to high European standards in regard to technological development and hence consider modernity more in this context.

However, although quantitative data identified that Arabs considered Berlin as more modern than Protestant Europeans did; qualitative collected data did not prove this. In actual terms, Arab interviewees partly contradicted Arab survey participants in this respect. Concerning qualitative data, Protestant Europeans considered Berlin as more modern, although many simultaneously refer to historical sites.

'Berlin is completely modern now...'

-Female, 23, UK-

'Berlin is a modern city...'

-Female, 19, Switzerland-

'Very European…historical buildings…old buildings'

-Male, 19, Saudi Arabia-

Although Arab survey respondents and Arab interviewees contradicted each other in this respect, the latter group's stance towards Berlin still differed from the one of Protestant Europeans.

Furthermore, this section's findings confirmed the findings of previous sections in terms of inner-cultural differences within Protestant European respondents. Again, Scandinavians agreed on average more with the destination attributes under functional holistic (Table 6.7) than Protestant Europeans from other countries and were more homogenous as a group.

Table 6.7: Average means of responses under functional holistic by nationality

UK = 2.6	Netherlands = 2.5	Germany = 2.6
Norway = 2.3	Denmark = 2.3	Sweden = 2.3

Both qualitative and quantitative data revealed cultural differences in the affective image of Berlin with Protestant Europeans having a better mental picture of Berlin. It is not only culture-specific in regard of the Arabs and Protestants, but inner-cultural differences also occurred within Protestant Europeans. Therefore, in terms of functional holistic factors concerning Berlin's destination image, there appears to be a correlation between cultural background and the image of the place.

6.7   Question 7: Psychological holistic picture of Berlin

The seventh question in the survey intended to capture participants' general feeling towards Berlin. On average, the attributes under psychological holistic had a mean value of 2.2, which means that respondents' general feeling towards Berlin was quite positive overall.

In order to identify the level of correlation between cultural background and perception of Berlin in terms of psychological holistic dimensions, an ANOVA test was conducted. The test revealed significant differences in just two of nine (22%) dimensions, which are highlighted in table 6.8. The low outcome of the ANOVA test questions the proposition that people's general feeling towards Berlin varies from culture to culture; particularly in consideration of the remaining dimensions, which were clearly beyond the significance level.

Table 6.8: One-way ANOVA test on the psychological holistic picture by cultural background

Between groups	Sum of Squares	F	Sig.
Pleasant	.891	2.359	.126
Lively/dynamic	3.294	6.065	.015
Exciting	.093	.139	.709
Entertaining	.004	.009	.927
Attractive	3.164	7.000	.009
Charming	.075	.088	.767
Trendy/cool	.135	.162	.688
Creative/innovative	1.385	1.960	.163
Good atmosphere for tourists	.596	.929	.336

However, qualitative data demonstrated apparent differences in this context. Like the outcomes of quantitative data, qualitative data showed that Protestant Europeans noticeably considered Berlin as more 'dynamic' and more 'attractive' as a tourist destination. As mentioned in previous sections, Arabs generally appeared to have a negative attitude towards Germans, which also reflects in their stance towards Berlin. Therefore, instead of associating Berlin with 'dynamic' or 'attractive', they rather consider Berlin as cold and not worthwhile to visit.

'One of my friends works for...in Berlin...and I'm planning to visit him, not for Berlin, but to visit my friend'

-Male, 23, Saudi Arabia-

'...anyway I don't feel myself attracted to Berlin'

-Female, 24, Jordan-

'... I'm not planning to go there'

-Male, 21, Kuwait-

'Berlin...cold. Not really sunny with serious...people'

-Male, 23, Saudi Arabia-

On the contrary, Protestant Europeans strikingly described Berlin more positively, which suggests that they consider Berlin as more attractive, more entertaining and generally a sound place for a tourist.

'New generation of young people, busy nightlife. Lots of entertainment but also the history of the city. Modern city with a big history'

-Female, 23, Netherlands-

One interviewee effectively represented the general attitude of Protestant Europeans. Her statement demonstrates that Berlin is perceived as an attractive tourist destination.

'Berlin is a modern city with a lot of attractions. There are lots of tourists everywhere. People drink beer and eat sausages in bars and cafes'

-Female, 19, Switzerland-

Furthermore, the general feeling towards the place remarkably appeared to fluctuate among Protestant European respondents, as well as among Arab-Islamic respondents. Once more, it emerged that Scandinavians were more inclined to find Berlin attractive as a tourist place compared to Britons, as additionally proved by the calculation of the mean values in table 6.9.

Table 6.9: Average means of responses under psychological holistic by nationality

UK = 2.3	Netherlands = 2.3	Germany = 2.2
Norway = 2.0	Denmark = 2.0	Sweden = 2.2

Qualitative data also established this occurrence, as illustrated by the following statements.

> *'Berlin is such a brilliant City and I'm definitely going there on my next holiday'*
>
> -Male, 25, Denmark-

> *'It's not a place that I would visit. But then you know if it comes to European countries, I think Germany is the last on my list that I would consider to visit'*
>
> -Female, 24, UK-

Britons yet seem to be severely influenced by the events of the Second World War, when expressing their overall feelings towards Germany. The British interviewee added that the war was still frequently broadcasted on British TV and that this may affect people's image of Germany, as shown in 6.5.

Among Arab respondents, statistically significant differences occurred between people from the UAE, whose feelings towards Berlin were blatantly positive, while the remaining Arabs felt the contrary (Table 6.10).

Table 6.10: Average means of responses under psychological holistic by Arab nationalities

UAE = 1.9	Egypt = 2.4	Jordan = 2.6
Qatar = 2.3	Saudi Arabia = 2.3	

This might be a repercussion of Berlin's marketing efforts in the UAE. BTM's (2006, p.82) marketing efforts in the Middle East put the greatest emphasis on the UAE, which may impinge on people's image of Berlin. Additionally, Germany's bilateral relations with the UAE are perceived to be the best in the Arab world, which is also reflected in regard to the economy. The UAE is Germany's largest trading partner in the Arab world (German Embassy 2007, Gulf Inside 2007), which may indirectly influence people's image of Berlin.

Perceptual differences did not only occur among Arab-Islamic and Protestant Europeans as a whole, but also between nationalities, which proves cross-cultural differences in this respect. Cross-cultural differences in Arab's and Protestant's general feelings towards Berlin were persuasively demonstrated by qualitative rather than by quantitative data. Since qualitative data is recognised to be more expressive where destination image constructs are studied (Molina & Esteban 2006), a correlation between cultural background and psychological holistic image of Berlin can be established.

6.8   How do you rate your overall image of Berlin as a tourist destination?

At the end of the questionnaire respondents were asked to assess their conclusive image of Berlin. The pie chart (Figure 6.5) illustrates that most respondents had a positive image (54%), 24% had a neutral, 15% a very positive and 8% a negative one. None of the respondents had a very negative image.

Figure 6.5: How do you rate your overall image of Berlin?

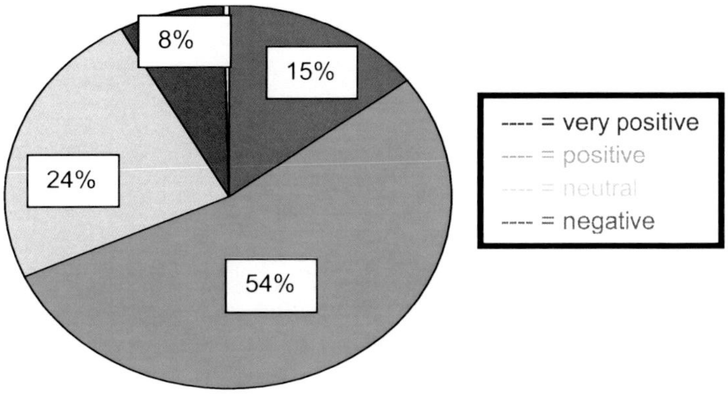

The findings of the questionnaire were subsequently cross-tabulated and an ANOVA test was conducted to identify potential cross-cultural deviations in individuals' assessments of Berlin's image. The cross-tabulation was indicative for cultural variations, since more Protestant Europeans than Arabs rated their image as positive, while, simultaneously, more Arabs than Protestant Europeans assessed their image as neutral and negative (Figure 6.6). This confirmed the propensity of Arabs to have a more negative stance towards Berlin, which emerged throughout this chapter.

Figure 6.6: Cross tabulation of the overall image of Berlin

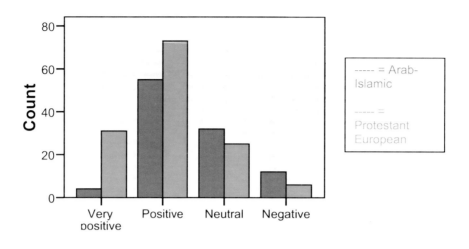

Besides, the ANOVA test established statistically highly significant cross-cultural differences, which are highlighted in table 6.11.

Table 6.11: One-way ANOVA test on the general perception of Berlin by cultural background

Between groups	Sum of Squares	F	Sig.
	12.385	21.259	.000

Qualitative data additionally verified this tendency. Generally, the researcher gained the impression that Arab interviewees were rather dismissive and negative and by far less enthusiastic than their counterparts regarding Berlin. It appeared that Berlin was simply not considered as an attractive tourist destination. Various statements of Arabs and Protestants that have been shown throughout this chapter have confirmed that Protestant Europeans had a more positive stance towards Berlin. When interviewees were asked to rate their overall image of the city, it became clear that relevant differences existed between the groups.

'Negative: I like activities, especially water activities, so my hobby is down in the Mediterranean not in the cold places'

-Male, 21, Kuwait-

'Very good: Very, very positive, very...'

-Female, 17, Norway-

This chapter also established perceptual differences within Protestant Europeans on a national level, which could also be confirmed in this part. Scandinavians were more homogenous as a sub-group and also more positive towards Berlin than other Protestants, especially Britons. The mean values in table 6.12 illustrate this.

Table 6.12: Average means of responses under psychological holistic by nationality

UK = 2.1	Netherlands = 2.1	Germany = 2.3
Norway = 1.7	Denmark = 1.9	Sweden = 1.8
UAE = 2.1	Egypt = 2.6	Jordan = 2.6
Qatar = 2.6	Saudi Arabia = 2.7	

The group interviews supported this tendency. Britons' general attitudes towards Germany was negative, which supports Wittlinger (2004) who claims that Britons' stance towards Germany can be regarded as malicious in many aspects of life, be it in sports, politics, economy or tourism. This seems to impact on Britons' Berlin image. Consequently, a British interviewee answered as following, when asked to rate her overall image of Berlin.

'Rather negative, it's not a place that I would visit. But then you know, if it comes to European countries I think Germany is the last on my list that I would consider to visit'

-Female, 24, UK-

However, perceptual differences did not only emerge among Protestants, but also among Arabs. For instance, respondents from the UAE evaluated their image of

Berlin as clearly more positive than Arabs of other nationalities (Table 6.13). The possible reason was already mentioned in 6.5. It seems that sound economic and political cooperation between Germany and the UAE influence people's image of Berlin.

Strikingly, Germans had the worst image of Berlin among Protestant Europeans. This might be due to the fact that the whole of Germany had to show plenty of economic solidarity towards Berlin for the regeneration of the city after the wall came down, but also due to Berlin being often broadcasted in national news for its increasing crime rate. Consequently, the media may provoke a negative Berlin image among Germans.

In terms of cultural differences in the perception of a place, it shows that information sources can have a huge impact on one's image of a place. Since they vary from country to country, it emerges that people from varying countries are differently influenced by media sources, for example, and develop different images, meaning that destination image is most likely to be culture-specific and may vary from country to country.

6.9   Summary

The knowledge gap that existed prior to this study could be filled. The analysis chapter evidently established a correlation of cultural background and the perception of Berlin as a tourist destination. Arab-Islamic youths' image of Berlin significantly differed from the image of youths from historically Protestant European countries in all four components that define destination image according to Echtner and Brent Ritchie (2003); namely individual functional destination attributes, psychological destination attributes, people's functional holistic- and psychological holistic picture. Figure 6.7 illustrates the destination image components and points where perceptual differences between the groups took place. The graphs for each cultural group in the diagram were formed according to statistical data and the mean values of each component.

The perceptual map demonstrates that statistically significant differences occurred regarding respondents' functional holistic picture, as well as the psychological holistic picture of Berlin with Arab respondents generally having a more negative picture and feeling towards Berlin. Furthermore, Arab respondents did not rate psychological and functional destination attributes concerning Berlin, as highly as Protestant Europeans did. Consequently, quantitative data proved that Arabs' overall image of the city was clearly more negative.

Figure 6.7: Perceptual mapping of Berlin's image between Arab-Islamic and Protestant European respondents

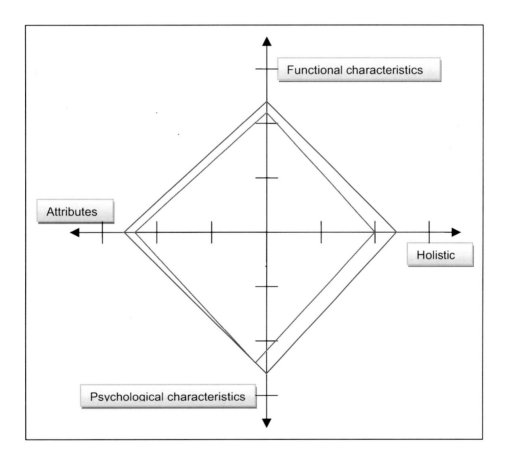

Arab-Islamic = ---------
Protestant European = ---------

Quantitative data did not always substantiate significant perceptual differences between the groups though. However, qualitative data, which is recognised to be more expressive than quantitative data where destination image constructs are studied (Molina & Esteban 2006), demonstrated obvious cross-cultural divergences in each of the destination image components. It provided sufficient evidence that Berlin's image is culture-specific.

Moreover, primary research also established inner-cultural differences among Protestant Europeans and partly among Arab-Islamic respondents. Scandinavians appeared to have a positive and homogenous image of Berlin, while Britons strikingly had a negative stance towards Berlin, most likely due to events of the Second World War. Clear tendencies among Dutch and German respondents could not be identified. Among Arab youths, adolescents from the UAE overall had a better feeling towards Berlin than Arabs of other nationalities. This might be due to exemplary bilateral relations between Germany and the UAE that could affect people's picture of a place. As a consequence, in the case of Britons and youths from the UAE, it became apparent that political events have a huge impact on the formation of image. For instance Britons regularly mentioned the War when referring to Berlin, which still affects people's image even 63 years after the War.

To conclude primary research suggests that a destination's image varies from one culture to another and may vary from one nation to another. The latter can even take place despite similar cultural backgrounds, as seen in the case of Protestant Europeans. In this, the nature of external factors in the direct environment of people plays a highly influential role. Overall, destination image is culture-specific.

Chapter Seven: Conclusion and recommendations

7.1   Introduction

Identifying whether there is a correlation between cultural background and the perception of Berlin, in an era referring to global tourists, has been the focal point of this exploratory study. Combined with the conceptual framework, the first chapter introduced the research background and presented the layout of this book and Chapters Two and Three provided additional background information on Berlin as a tourist destination. Subsequently, Chapters Four and Five reviewed preceding literature on destination image and influential factors, as well as the effects of globalisation on consumer behaviour. The Arab-Islamic and Protestant European cultures and youth cultures were also examined. Nevertheless, the literature review could not solve the research question, so primary research was required, which was explained in Chapter Five. Chapter Six presented the most relevant primary research findings and fulfilled the research question. All research objectives could be completed. Finally, this chapter discusses the main findings and gives recommendations for the industry. The final part of this chapter provides recommendations for further research.

7.2   Discussions and conclusions

This book has made a significant contribution to the comprehension of the possible effects of globalisation on consumers' perceptions of Berlin as a tourist destination in the context of a cross-cultural study. Despite the growing internationality of tourism and the image's vital role in destination management, cross-cultural studies are scarce, especially in this field. In the light of globalisation, which is frequently considered as homogenising cultures (Buttaro 2005, CATO Institute 2003, Chang *et al.* 2006, Isizoh 2006, Redford & Brosius 2006) as well as their tastes and preferences, the lack of cross-cultural studies regarding destination image rendered it reasonable to explore this topic.

However, a few previous studies have studied the impact of culture on the formation of the image of a place. Some did not identify significant correlations between cultural background and perception of a place (Chaudary 2000, MacKay and Fesenmaier 2000), whereas the majority did and established that the image formation process underlies cultural factors (Beerli & Martin 2004, Kee-Fu Tsang & Ap 2007, Kozak *et al.* 2004, Mattila 2000, Reisinger & Turner 2002a, Truong & King 2006,

Zhao 2006). They obtain empirical support to this contentious debate by this study. Regardless of the massive wave of globalisation, which tends to affect younger generations in particular (Pelkington *et al.* 2002, Zahid 2007), the results indicate that youth from diverse cultural backgrounds perceive a place such as Berlin differently (Figure 7.1).

In each of the four components of destination image utilised to measure Arab-Islamic and Protestant Europeans' image of Berlin, the focus groups showed significant differences. Arab-Islamic survey participants overall had a more negative stance towards Berlin than did Protestant Europeans. It may be that Arab youths progressively absorb Western values and lifestyles as stated by Rayappa (2005), but this has so far not caused homogenous perceptions of a place between the groups. Consequently, the findings signify that globalisation does not have a homogenising effect on individuals' perception of a place. For destination managers, this means that tourist markets cannot be treated homogenously in this context due to cross-cultural differences in tastes and preferences.

The phenomenon of the *'distance factor'*, which recognises that people receive less information about a destination the further away they live from the it (Blackwell *et al.* 2001 cited Zhao 2006, Frochot & Legohere 2007, p.184), appears to be one of the reasons for heterogeneous perceptions of a place on a cross-cultural scale. This study provides support to this stance. It was established that youth from an Arab-Islamic background had a distorted image of Berlin and rather referred to Germany when assessing Berlin, while most Protestant Europeans had a distinct notion and more complex picture of the city. This phenomenon also induced cross-cultural differences in the perceptions of Berlin. As a consequence, to enhance its image in the Arab World, Berlin would need to promote itself there to stimulate a distinct picture among the population rather than having itself promoted by third parties that market Berlin in conjunction with Germany and other German destinations. Nonetheless, this does still not mean that Arab-Islamic people would perceive Berlin as Protestant Europeans do.

Apart from this, the study has made some further interesting findings. A previous study by Inglehart (cited Inglehart & Baker 2000) examined different regions and ethnicities by their cultural context and established that Northern/Western European countries, including the UK, share the Protestant culture. Thus, they share similar values and beliefs and demonstrate common behavioural patterns in terms of *'thinking, feeling and acting'* (Hofstede 1991 cited van Egmond 2005, p.19). However, in terms of Protestant European youths' feelings towards Berlin, this study noted remarkable inner-cultural deviations, which may question the validity of Inglehart's clustering of Northern/Western European countries. Statistical data revealed that Germans and Dutch were very similar in evaluating Berlin's destination attributes, while Britons were noticeably less affirmative. Strikingly though, Scandinavians acted most homogenously throughout the collection of primary data and had more positive attitudes towards Berlin than did Britons and slightly more than the Dutch and Germans.

It was concluded that people from countries that were particularly affected by the Second World War, such as the Netherlands and the UK, had a particular attitude towards Germany. This does not have to mean that Protestant Europeans overall differ in their thinking and feeling, but differences could be established concerning their feelings towards Germany. Besides, this point demonstrates that destination image does not only vary between cultures, but may vary between nations. Consequently, Berlin's tourist authorities are advised to apply additional marketing strategies in order to enhance the city's image in the UK and the Netherlands. Even though these markets are already Berlin's main source markets, such a strategy could further stimulate the number of inbound tourists from these countries.

A further point vindicates the latter recommendation. This study provides support to Stern and Krakover (1993) who empirically proved that affective components of destination image severely influence perceptive/cognitive components. The majority of Arab and British youth appeared to have negative emotional feelings towards Berlin and consequently rated Berlin's destination attributes lower than other survey participants. Strikingly, Germans were often regaded as unfriendly, which impinges on people's feeling towards Berlin. Thus, it is recommended to raise awareness among Berliners in regard of the importance of tourism and the potential benefits to the city in order to stimulate more amicable attitudes, which may bring about postive effects to the city's tourism industry. Additionally, further PR and other marketing tools in the above-mentioned places could improve people's emotional feelings towards Berlin, so that they might be more inclined to evaluate the city's attributes higher. As a result more people might also be attracted to visit Berlin.

From a practical standpoint this appears difficult, since Arab and British organic images of Berlin are apparently negatively influenced by their direct external environment, such as the media. Growing hostility of the Arab world towards the West is confronted by a chronological malicious attitude of Britons towards Germany, which aggravates this task. However, Frochot and Legohére (2007, p.179-180) signify that people living further away from a destination are likely to be quite influenced by the induced type of image, as they might not have a clear image of the destination, and this could facilitate the modification of the image in the Arab World. Since British interviewees also appeared to have a blurred picture of Berlin, it is likely that their image could also be modified through increased promotion of the city's destination attributes with a particular focus on changing the image from the German stereotype of the unfriendly and cold person. Berlin has changed over recent decades, also in this context.

Figure 7.1: Summary of main outcomes

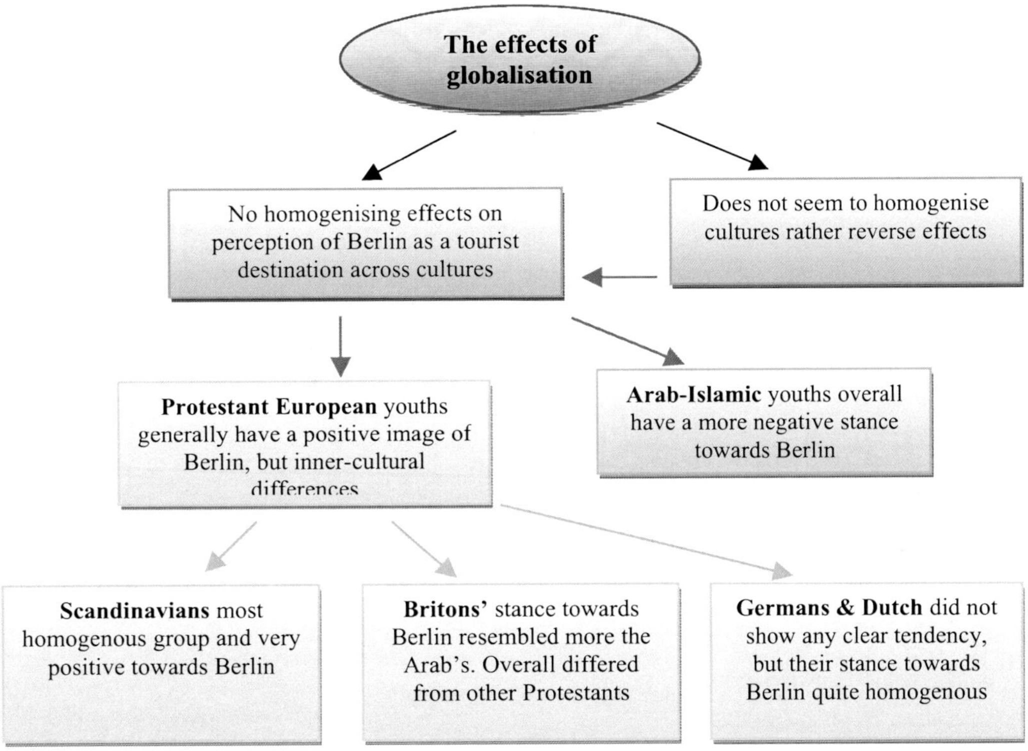

To conclude, it emerged that Berlin's image as a tourist destination varies across cultures and partly across nations that share the same culture (Figure 7.1). Especially, in Britain and in the Arab World, Berlin's image appears to be negative among youth, so it is recommended that measures be implemented to improve the city's image accordingly. The massive wave of globalisation has so far not homogenised people's perception of a place across cultures. Consequently, the research question can be answered. In an era referring to the global tourist, Berlin's tourist authorities have still to consider cultural segmentation when developing marketing strategies relating to the place's image.

7.3 Recommendations for further research

At present, a limited number of destination image studies exist that are based on identifying correlations between cultural background and perception of a place. The on-going globalisation process might make it imperative to research this area in more depth.

Recommendations must be made with regard to issues of methodology.

Firstly, this research project studied the destination image of a German city, which has a particular status regarding the Second World War; hence, individuals' images of this place might be biased. In order to establish the findings of this study, it is recommended that similar studies be conducted but in more neutral destinations. Moreover, choosing Berlin as a case study to scrutinise whether destination image varied between cultures was disadvantageous, as it has no world reputation unlike New York, London or Paris. People from distant places might simply have a blurred image of Berlin, because they know little about it, while the distance factor might be weaker with other metropolises.

Secondly, it is recommended to extend the number of cultures being compared to accomplish more expressive results where destination image's culture-specificity is studied. Further research should increase the sample size, so that each cultural background is represented by unbiased samples.

Thirdly, this study ignored the effects of other influential factors on image formation, such as age, education or gender for instance, which could be analysed in conjunction with cultural factors in order to obtain better understanding of tourist behaviour.

Finally, this research focalised on finding out individuals' destination image at the pre-visitation stage. However, the process of destination image additionally incorporates in-destination and post-visitation images. Thus, further research should, ideally, be ongoing, in which survey participants are interviewed at each of the stages.

7.4 Summary

This chapter has discussed primary research findings with existing literature and simultaneously provided recommendations for Berlin's tourist authorities before giving recommendations for further research. Furthermore, it has answered the research question. A correlation between cultural background and perception of a place could not be established. Consequently, in an era referring to the global tourist, Berlin's tourist authorities have still to consider cultural segmentation when developing marketing strategies relating to the place's image.

Bibliography

Abi-Saab, P. (2005). Interviewed by: Hijazi, Y. *'Arab Culture under Threat before Globalisation'*. Germany: Qantara Dialogue with the Islamic World. Available from: http://www.qantara.de/webcom/show_article.php/_c-327/_nr-18/_p-1/i.html. (Accessed 27/07/2008).

Adjouri Brand Consultants GmbH (2008). *Factsheet Pressekonferenz/Pressefruehstueck* [online]. Berlin Tourism Marketing GmbH. Available from: http://www.berlin-tourist-information.de/bilder/presse/download/BTM_Adjouri_Factsheet.pdf. (Accessed 22/07/2008).

Albaum, G. (1997). The Likert scale revisited: an alternate version. (product preference testing). *Journal of the Market Research Society*. 39 (2), pp.331-343.

Al-Ghanim, M.H. (2005). *Arab Youth and WPAY, Challenges and Success 1995-2005: A Regional Overview* [online]. Egypt: Global Youth Action Network. Available from: http://www.un.org/esa/socdev/unyin/documents/wpaysubmissions/gyan_arab_region.pdf. (Accessed 19/07/2008).

Al-Hamarneh, Dr.A. (2006). Arab Medical Tourism in Germany. *Islamic Tourism*. 21, pp.20-22.

Al Lawati, A., Habib, R. and Al Theeb, A. (2007). *Arab youth redefine individuality* [online]. Gulfnews. Available from: http://archive.gulfnews.com/articles/07/03/03/10108321.html. (Accessed 29/07/2008).

Altwaijri, Dr. A.O. (1998). *The Arab Culture and other Cultures* [online]. Ryadh: Publications of the Islamic Educational, Scientific and Cultural Organization, ISESCO. Available from: http://jeunessearabe.info/IMG/Arab_culture_and_other_cult-en.pdf. (Accessed 16/07/2008).

Al-Twaijri, M. and Al-Muhaiza, I.A. (2004). Hofstede's cultural dimensions in the GCC countries: An empirical investigation. *International Journal of Value-Based Management.* 9 (2), pp. 121-131.

Al-Wugayan, A.A. (2004). An Empirical Investigation of Consumer Ethics in a Collectivist Arab Culture: Consumer-Retailer Relationship (CRR) Approach. *Journal of International Consumer Marketing.* 16 (3), pp. 25-54.

Ateljevic, I. (1999). Tourist Motivation, Values and Perceptions. In: Woodside, A.G., Crouch, G.I., Mazanec, J.A., Oppermann, M. And Sakai, M.Y., ed. *Consumer Psychology of Tourism, Hospitality and Leisure.* CABI Publishing, pp.193-209.

Baden-Fuller, C.W.F. and Stopford, J.M. (1991). Globalization Frustrated: The Case of White Goods. *Strategic Management Journal.* 12 (7), pp.493-507.

Baloglu, S. (1999). A Path-Analytical Model of Visitation Intention Involving Information Sources, Socio-Psychological Motivations and Destination Images. In: Woodside, A.G., Crouch, G.I., Mazanec, J.A., Oppermann, M. And Sakai, M.Y., ed. *Consumer Psychology of Tourism, Hospitality and Leisure.* CABI Publishing, pp.63-90.

Baloglu, S. And McCleary, K.W. (1999). A MODEL OF DESTINATION IMAGE FORMATION. *Annals of Tourism Research.* 25 (4), pp.858-897.

Beerli, A. and Martin, J.D. (2004). FACTORS INFLUENCING DESTINATION IMAGE. *Annals of Tourism Research.* 31 (3), pp.657-681.

Belk, R.W. (1996). Hyperreality and Globalization: Culture in the Age of Ronald Mc Donald. *Journal of International Consumer Marketing.* 8 (3/4), pp.23-37.

Bell, D. (1987). Acts of Union: Youth Sub-Culture and Ethnic Identity amongst Protestants in Northern Ireland. *The British Journal of Sociology.* 38 (2), pp.158-183.

Benedict XVI (2006). *Europe and Its Discontents* [online]. First Things: The Journal of Religion, Culture, And Public Life. Available from: http://www.firstthings.com/article.php3?id_article=70. (Accessed 29/07/2008).

Bertelsmann Stiftung (2008). *World's youth more religious than reputed* [online]. Germany, Guetersloh: Bertelsmann Stiftung. Available from: http://www.bertelsmann-stiftung.de/cps/rde/xchg/SID-0A000F0A-15DBAB1F/bst_engl/hs.xsl/nachrichten_88550.htm. (Accessed 29/07/2008).

Berkowitz, S. (1997). *Analyzing Qualitative Data, What Is Qualitative Analysis?* [online]. USA, National Science Foundation. Available from: http://www.ehr.nsf.gov/EHR/REC/pubs/NSF97-153/CHAP_4.HTM [Accessed 22/01/2008].

Birkeland, I. and Isaksen, A. (2007). *Culture Economy and Tourism* [online]. Available from: http://www.uib.no/ngm/content/CultureEconomyTourism.pdf. (Accessed 02/07/2008).

Black, N. (2007). *Protestant Countries Have Higher Employment Rates* [online]. The Christian Post. Available from: http://www.christianpost.com/article/20071003/study-protestant-countries-have-higher-employment-rates.htm. (Accessed 28/07/2008).

BPB (2005). *Das Image Deutschlands im Ausland* [online]. Bundeszentrale fuer politische Bildung. Available from: http://www.bpb.de/methodik/CPT1QE,0,0,M_01_05_Das_Image_Deutschlands_im_Ausland.html. (Accessed 29/07/2008).

Blaxter, L, Hughes, C. and Tight, M. (2001), *HOW TO research.* Second edition. Buckingham: Open University Press.

Brooklyn College (1999). *The Shaping of the Modern World. Section1: Roots of Western Culture* [online]. USA: Brooklyn College. Available from: http://academic.brooklyn.cuny.edu/history/virtual/core4-1.htm. (Accessed 15/08/2008).

BTM (2006). *Berlin zum Erfolg 2006-2010 Strategische Marketingplanung.* Berlin: Berlin Tourismus Marketing GmbH.

BTM (2007). *Did you know that…? 50 interesting facts and figure on the German capital* [online]. Berlin: Berlin Tourismus Marketing GmbH. Available from: http://www.visitberlin.de/english/presse/download-basistexte/e_pr_basistext_facts-figures_2007.pdf. (Accessed 14/08/2008).

BTM (2008a). *Berlin Tourism Reaches New Heights in 2007* [online]. Berlin: Berlin Tourismus Marketing GmbH. Available from: http://www.visitberlin.de/english/presse/download/e_pr_317_tourism-2007.pdf. (Accessed 30/07/2008).

BTM (2008b). *Statistik Januar bis Dezember 2007* [online]. Berlin: Berlin Tourismus Marketing GmbH. Available from: http://www.berlin-tourist-information.de/partnerforum/images/stories/download/d_pf_statistik_dezember_200 7.pdf. (Accessed 31/07/2008).

Buda, R. (1998). Cultural Differences between Arabs and Americans. *Journal of Cross-Cultural Psychology.* 29 (3), pp.487-492.

Buttaro, A. (2005). *Sticking Up For Globalization* [online]. Boston: BCHEIGHTS.com The Independent Student Newspaper of Boston College. Available from: http://media.www.bcheights.com/media/storage/paper144/news/2005/04/04/Marketplace/Sticking.Up.For.Globalization-911032-page2.shtml. (Accessed 16/07/2008).

Cathy, H.C., Wolfe, K. And Kang, S.K. (2004). Image assessment for a destination with limited comparative advantages. *Tourism Management.* 25 (1), pp. 121-126.

CATO Institute (2003). Globalization and Culture [online]. Washington: CATO Policy Report Vol. XXV No.3. Available from: http://www.cato.org/pubs/policy_report/v25n3/cpr-25n3.pdf. (Accessed 30/07/2008).

Chang, J.H., Chen, G.M, Heisey, D.R., Miike, Y. Nesbitt, T., de la Peza, C., Servaes, J., Shi, X. (2006). Intercultural Symposium on Cultural Globalization. *China Media Research*. 2 (3), pp. 100-105.

Chaudary, M. (2000). India's image as a tourist destination – a perspective of foreign tourists. *Tourism Management*. 21 (3), pp. 293-297.

Cherkaoui, N. (2007). *New report addresses causes of sex tourism in Morocco* [online]. Rabat: Magharebia. Available from: http://www.magharebia.com/cocoon/awi/xhtml1/en_GB/features/awi/features/2007/1 2/28/feature-01. (Accessed 29/07/2008).

Choi, S., Lehto, X.Y. and Morrison, A.M. (2007). Destination image representation on the web: Content analysis of Macau travel related websites. *Tourism Management*. 28 (1), pp.118-129.

Chon, K.-S. (1990). The Role of Destination Image in Tourism: A Review and Discussion. *The Tourist Review*. 2, pp.2-9.

Clark, G. (2008). *Super Star Cities?* [online]. ULI Europe Conference. Available from: www.uli.org/Content/ContentGroups/Events/Conferences/Europe2008/SuperstarCiti esGregClark.ppt. (Accessed 30/07/2008).

Cooper, C., Fletcher, J., Fyall, A., Gilbert, D. & Wanhill, S. (2005). *Tourism Principles and Practice*. 3rd ed. Madrid: Mateu Como Artes Graficas

Coshall, J.T. (2000). Measurement of tourist's images: The repertory grid approach. *Journal of Travel Research*. 39 (1), pp.85-89.

Deutsche Welle (2004). *Examining Germany's Image Abroad* [online]. Germany: DW-World.de. Available from: http://www.dw-world.de/dw/article/0,2144,1232956,00.html. (Accessed 02/08/2008).

Delacroix, J. and Nielsen, F. (2001). The Beloved Myth: Protestantism and the Rise of Industrial Capitalism in Nineteenth-Century Europe. *Social Forces.* 80 (2), pp.509-553.

De Mooij, M. (2004). *Consequences for Global Marketing and Advertising.* London: Sage Pub.

Di Marino, E. (2007). *The Strategic Dimension of Destination Image. An Analysis of the French Riviera Image from the Italian Tourists' Perceptions.* Thesis (PHD). University of Naples ''Federico II'' Faculty of Economics.

Echtner, C.M. and Brent Ritchie, J.R. (2003). The Meaning and Measurement of Destination Image. *The Journal of Tourism Studies.* 14 (1), pp.37-48.

Eitzen, D.S. and Baca Zinn, M. (2006). *Globalization The Transformation of Social Worlds.* USA: Thomas Higher Education.

El-Gawhary, K. (1995). Sex Tourism in Cairo. *Middle East Report.* 25 (5), pp.26-27.

Emery, J. (2008). *Arab Culture and Muslim Stereotypes* [online]. Washington D.C.: Middle East Times. Available from: http://www.metimes.com/Opinion/2008/06/17/arab_culture_and_muslim_stereotypes/5948/. (Accessed 14/07/2008).

ETN (2008). *Egypt battles 'sex tourism', bans 92-year-old from marrying teen* [online]. ETN Global Travel Industry News. Available from: http://www.eturbonews.com/3086/egypt-battles-sex-tourism-bans-92-year-old-ma. (Accessed 29/07/2008).

Fakeye, P.C. and Crompton, J.R. (1991). ''Image Differences between Prospective, First-Time and Repeat Visitors to the Lower Rio Grande Valley''. *Journal of Travel Research.* 30 (2), pp.10-16.

Fasman, J. (2003). *Freedom Coke The Arab World's Foolish Boycott of American Food* [online]. USA: Slate Magazine. Available from: http://www.slate.com/id/2080611/. (Accessed 27/07/2008).

FAZ (2008). *Studie ueber Reiseziele: Oslo und Kopenhagen sind teurste Staedte der Welt* [online]. Germany: Frankfurter Allgemeine. Available from: http://www.faz.net/s/RubCD175863466D41BB9A6A93D460B81174/Doc~E066B75 512D3544428F338935A6EC51F0~ATpl~Ecommon~Scontent.html. (Accessed 14/08/2008).

Fisher, C. (2004). *Researching and Writing a Dissertation For Business Students.* UK: Ashford Colour Press Ltd.

Finucane, J.J. (2008). *Western Culture and the Arab World* [online]. New York: New York Times. Available from: http://query.nytimes.com/gst/fullpage.html?res=9C03E4DF163DF933A25751C0A9 649C8B63. (Accessed 15/07/2008).

Flatau, S. (2008). *Berlin ist auch bei schlechtem Wetter beliebt* [online]. Berlin: Berliner Morgenpost. Available from: http://www.morgenpost.de/printarchiv/berlin/article170175/Berlin_ist_auch_bei_schl echtem_Wetter_beliebt.html. (Accessed 23/03/2008).

Focus (1994). *Berlin-Image Endlich wachgeworden* [online]. Focus Online. Available from: http://www.focus.de/politik/deutschland/berlin-image-endlich-wachgeworden_aid_145061.html. (Accessed 21/06/2008).

Font, X. (1996). Managing the tourist destination's image. *Journal of Vacation Marketing.* 3 (2), pp.123-131.

Friedman, T. (1995). *The World Is Flat: A Brief History of the Globalized World in the Twenty-first Century.* USA: Allen Lane.

Frochot, I. and Legohere, L. (2007). *Le Marketing du tourisme.* Paris: Dunod

Frost, R. (2006). *As the World Flattens. Does globalization threaten or nurture local markets?* [online]. Available from: http://www.businessweek.com/innovate/content/jun2006/id20060621_139874.htm?chan=globalbiz_europe_around+the+globe. (Accessed 27/07/2008).

Fukuyama, Dr.F. (1998). Interviewed by: Merrill Lynch Forum. *Economic Globalization and Culture* [online]. Available from: http://www.ml.com/woml/forum/pdfs/Fuku_iview.pdf. (Accessed 27/07/2008).

Galal, Dr.A., Galander, Dr.M. and Auter, Dr.P. (2008). *The Image of the United States Portrayed in Arab World Online Journalism.* USA: The University of Louisana at Lafayette.

Gartner, W.C. (1993). Image formation process. *Journal of Travel and Tourism Marketing.* 2(2), pp. 191-215.

Gavlak, D. (2008). *Arab education 'falling behind'* [online]. Amman: BBC News. Available from: http://news.bbc.co.uk/1/hi/world/middle_east/7227610.stm. (Accessed 18/07/2008).

Geoghegan, T. (2006). *Berlin gets into World Cup mode* [online]. UK: BBC World News. Available from: http://news.bbc.co.uk/2/hi/europe/4897642.stm. (Accessed 04/08/2008).

German Embassy (2007). *Deutschland und die Vereinigten Arabischen Emirate* [online]. Abu Dhabi: German Embassy. Available from: http://www.abu-dhabi.diplo.de/Vertretung/abudhabi/de/Startseite.html. (Accessed 10/08/2008).

German Embassy (2008). *Deutschland und Saudi-Arabien* [online]. Riyadh: Deutsche Botschaft. Available from: http://www.riad.diplo.de/Vertretung/riad/de/03/Bilaterale__Beziehungen/seite__bilaterale__beziehungen.html. (Accessed 29/07/2008).

Gilner, J.A and Morgan, G.A. (2000). *Research Methods in applied settings. An integrated approach to design and analysis.* USA: Lawrence Erlbaum Associates.

Gnoth, J., Zins, A., Lengmueller, R. and Boshoff, C. (1999). The Relationship Between Emotions, Mood and Motivation to Travel: Towards a Cross-Cultural Measurement of Flow. In: Woodside, A.G., Crouch, G.I., Mazanec, J.A.,

Oppermann, M. And Sakai, M.Y., ed. *Consumer Psychology of Tourism, Hospitality and Leisure.* CABI Publishing, pp.155-176.

GNTB (2006). *Fussball-WM befluegelt Image des Reiselandes Deutschland* [online]. Frankfurt: Deutsche Zentrale fuer Tourismus. Available from: http://www.germany-tourism.de/pdf/PM_DZT_FIFA-D-Image_Ausland_Dez_06.pdf.　　　(Accessed 30/07/2008).

GNTB (2007). *Marktinformation Arabische Golfstaaten 2007.* Asien: Deutsche Zentrale fuer Tourismus. Available from: http://www.deutschland-extranet.de/pdf/MI_arab._Laender_2007(1).pdf. (Accessed 16/06/2008).

GNTB (2008). *German National Tourist Board Marketing and Sales for 'Destination Germany'* [online]. Frankfurt: Deutsche Zentrale fuer Tourismus. Available from: http://www.germany-tourism.de/pdf/DZT_MarketingFolder_en_web.pdf. (Accessed 29/07/2008).

Gruber, D. (Doreen.gruber@btm.de), 6th August 2008. *RE: Diplomarbeit.* E-mail to El Kadhi, W., (welkadhi@gmail.com).

Gulf Inside (2007). *Deutsche Spezialisten sind gefragt* [online]. Germany: A Maysmedia Publication. Available from: http://dev.port2.customer.j32.de/gulfinsidetv/archiv/1/download.pdf. (Accessed 10/08/2008).

Habermann, Dr. D., Schuck-Wersig, Dr. P., Angermeyer, A., Nowak, L. and Rahn, K. (2006). *Imagebefragung: Tourismusstandort Berlin in seiner bezirklichen Vielfalt. Studie 2006. Handlungsvorschlaege fuer ein multidimensionales Marketing* [online]. Berlin: Kombi Consult GmbH. Available from: http://www.berlin.de/imperia/md/content/senatsverwaltungen/senwaf/publikationen/imagebefragung_tourismus.pdf. (Accessed 04/07/2008).

Halsall, P. (1998). *Modern Western Civilization. Class 2: Roots of Western History* [online]. New York: Fordham University The Jesuit University of New York. Available from: http://www.fordham.edu/halsall/mod/lect/mod02.html. (Accessed 11/08/2008).

Halter, M. (1995). *New Migrants in the Marketplace: Boston's Ethnic Entrepreneurs.* USA: University of Massachusetts Press.

Hanlan, J. And Kelly, S. (2005). Image formation, information sources and an iconic Australian tourist destination. *Journal of Vacation Marketing.* 11 (2), pp.162-177.

Hedorfer, P. (2008). *Chancen fuer die touristische Vermarktung des Reiselandes Deutschland* [online]. Stuttgart: Deutsche Zentrale fuer Tourismus e.V. Available from: http://www.tourismus-bw.de/sixcms/media.php/33/Deutsche%20Zentrale%20f%C3%BCr%20Tourismus_Petra%20Hedorfer.pdf. (Accessed 29/07/2008).

Hofstede, G. (2001). *Culture's Consequences Comparing Values, Behaviors, Institutions and Organizations Across Nations.* USA: Sage Publications, Inc.

Hofstede, G. (2003). *Geert Hofstede Cultural Dimensions* [online]. The Netherlands: ITIM International. Available from: http://www.geert-hofstede.com/hofstede_arab_world.shtml. (Accessed 17/07/2008).

Hosany, S., Ekinci, Y. and Uysal, M. (2007). Destination Image and Destination Personality. *International Journal of Culture, Tourism and Hospitality Research.* 1 (1), pp. 62-81.

Hunt, J.D. (1975). Image as a factor in tourism development. *Journal of Travel Research.* 13 (3), pp. 1-7.

Inglehart, R. (1997). *Modernization and Postmodernization. Cultural, Economic, and Political Change in 43 Societies.* USA: Princeton University Press.

Inglehart. R. and Baker, W.E. (2000). Modernization, Cultural Change, and the Persistence of Traditional Values. *American Sociological Review.* 65 (1), pp.19-51.

Inglehart, R. and Welzel, C. (2005). *Modernization, Cultural Change, and Democracy. The Human Development Sequence.* Cambridge: Cambridge University Press.

ISESCO (2008). *The concept of cultural and educational* strategy [online]. Amman: Islamic Educational, Scientific and Cultural Organization. Available from: http://www.isesco.org.ma/english/publications/strategy/Chap6.php.   (Accessed 16/07/2008).

Isizoh, C.D. (2006) Globalisation of Cultures: Gains and Losses from an African Perspective. *In*: C. Ozankom and C. Udeani, ed. *Globalisation Cultures Religion.* Netherlands: Rodopi, pp. 145-150.

Jenkins, O.H. (1999). Understanding and measuring tourists' destination images. *International Journal of Tourism Research 1*, pp.1-15.

Johns, D. (2007). *Agreement signed with UNWTO to boost Youth Tourism* [online]. World Youth Student & Educational Travel. Available from: http://www.aboutwysetc.org/Communications.aspx#UNWTOsigning.   (Accessed 15/07/2008).

Kang, M. and Moscardo, G. (2006). Exploring Cross-cultural Differences in Attitudes towards Responsible Tourist Behaviour: A Comparison of Korean, British and Australian Tourists. *Asia Pacific Journal of Tourism Research.* 11 (4), pp. 304-320.

Kanniainen, V. and Pääkkönen, J. (2007). *Do the Catholic and Protestant Countries Differ by Their Tax Morale* [online]. Helsinki Center of Economic Research. Available from: http://ethesis.helsinki.fi/julkaisut/eri/hecer/disc/145/dothecat.pdf. (Accessed 28/07/2008).

Karasek, H. (2003). *Bundeslaender-Serie: Berlin* [online]. Deutschland Online. Available from: http://www.magazine-deutschland.de/bland/Berlin_6-03_ENG_E1.php?hdpfad=3. (Accessed 23/07/2008).

Kateregga, B.D. and Shenk, D.W. (1997). *A Muslim and a Christian in Dialogue Islam and Christianity.* Nairobi: Uzima Press.

Kee-Fu Tsang, N. and Ap, J. (2007). Tourists' Perceptions of Relational Quality Service Attributes: A Cross-Cultural Study. *Journal of Travel Research.* 10, pp.355-363.

Keller, A.S. and Stewart, G. (2005) *Protestant Europe: Its Crisis and Outlook.* USA: Kessinger Publishing.

Kim, H. and Richardson, S.L. (2003). Motion Pictures Impacts on Destination Images. *Annals of Tourism Research.* 30 (1), pp.216-237.

Knox, N. (2005). *Religion takes a back seat in Western Europe* [online]. USA: USA Today. Available from: http://www.usatoday.com/news/world/2005-08-10-europe-religion-cover_x.htm. (Accessed 17/07/2008).

Kozak, M., Bigne, E. and Andreu, L. (2003). Limitations of Cross-Cultural Customer Satisfaction Research and Recommending Alternative Methods. *Current Issues and Development in Hospitality and Tourism Satisfaction.* 4 (3), pp.37-59.

Kozak, M., Bigne, E., Gonzalez, A. and Andreu, L. (2004). Cross-Cultural behaviour research in tourism: a case study on destination image. *Tourism Analysis.* 8, pp.253-257.

Lashbrook, A.M. (1969). Latin: The Basic Language. *The Classical Journal.* 64 (4), pp.162-166.

Levitt, T. (1983). *The globalization of markets* [online]. Victoria University of Wellington. Available from: http://www.vuw.ac.nz/~caplabtb/m302w08/Levitt.pdf. (Accessed 26/07/2008).

Lonely Planet (2008). *Berlin: Overview – Cutting-edge Berlin is a feast of history, theatre and music* [online]. Lonely Planet Publications. Available from: http://www.lonelyplanet.com/worldguide/germany/berlin/. (Accessed 12/08/2008).

Long, J. (2007). *Researching Leisure, Sport and Tourism. The Essential Guide.* Great Britain: The Cromwell Press Ltd.

Lubbe, B. (2004). Applying an open systems public relations model to destination image development. *Communicatio.* 30 (1), pp.131-150.

MacKay, J. and Fesenmaier, D.R. (2000). An Exploration of Cross-Cultural Destination Image Assessment. *Journal of Travel Research.* 38 (4), pp. 417-423.

Macleod, D. (2004). *Tourism, Globalization and Cultural Change: An Island Community Perspective.* Toronto: Channel View Publications.

Madrigal, R. and Kahle, L.R. (1994). Predicting vacation activity preferences on the basis of value-system segmentation. *Journal of Travel Research.* 32 (3), pp. 22-28.

Mansfield, P. (2003). *A History of the Middle East.* England: Clays Ltd.

Maschewski, A. (2008a). *Touristen wollen mehr Mauer sehen* [online]. Berliner Morgenpost 04/03/2008. Available from: http://www.morgenpost.de/content/2008/03/04/berlin/950238.html. (Accessed 30/07/2008).

Maschewski, A. (2008b). *Berlin wird zum Catwalk* [online]. Berlin: Berliner Morgenpost. Available from: http://www.morgenpost.de/berlin/article704110/Jetzt_kommt_Berlin_in_Mode.html. (Accessed 27/07/2008).

Matsumoto, D., Grissom, R.J. and Dinnel, D.L. (2001). DO BETWEEN-CULTURE DIFFERENCES REALLY MEAN THAT PEOPLE ARE DIFFERENT? A Look of Some Measures of Cultural Effect Size. *Journal of Cross-Cultural Psychology.* 32 (4), pp. 478-490.

Mattila, A.S. (2000). The Impact of Culture and Gender on Customer Evaluations of Service Encounters. *Journal of Hospitality & Tourism Research.* 24 (2), pp.263-273.

Maussen, M. (2005). *Making Muslim Presence Meaningful* [online]. The Netherlands: Amsterdam School for Social science Research. Available from: http://www.assr.nl/workingpapers/documents/ASSR-WP0503.pdf. (Accessed 04/08/2008).

Mintel Marketing Intelligence (2004). *Outbound Travel – Middle East.* International: Mintel International Group.

Mintel Marketing Intelligence (2006a). *Youth Travel Market.* International: Mintel International Group.

Mintel Marketing Intelligence (2006b). *Middle East Outbound.* International: Mintel International Group.

Mintel Marketing Intelligence (2006c). *Youth Travel Market – International.* International: Mintel International Group.

Molina, A. and Esteban, A. (2006). Tourism Brochures Usefulness and Image. *Annals of Tourism Research.* 33 (4), pp.1036-1056.

Murphy, A. E. (2003). Illustrating the Utility of a Modified Gap Analysis as a Regional Tourism Planning Tool: Potential Japanese and German Travlers to the Cowichan Region. *Journal of Travel Research.* 41 (4), pp.400-409.

Naisbitt, J. (1994). *Global Paradox.* New York: William Morrow & Co..

Newman, T. (2004). *US Patent 6795084 – Heuristic determination of color reproduction parameters* [online]. Available from: http://www.patentstorm.us/patents/6795084/description.html. (Accessed 03/07/2008).

Nuscheler, F. (2006). Globalisierung. Begriffe – Dimensionen – Herausforderungen. *In*: C. Ozankom and C. Udeani, ed. *Globalisation Cultures Religion.* Netherlands: Rodopi, pp. 129-143.

OECD (2006). *Glossary of Statistical Terms* [online]. Organisation for Economic Co-operation and Development. Available from: http://stats.oecd.org/glossary/detail.asp?ID=120. (Accessed 21/07/2008).

Oneclimate.net (2007). *Recycling in the Arab World* [online]. London: One World UK. Available from: http://www.morainevalley.edu/ctl/MiddleEast/images/Map_Arab%20World%202.jpg. (Accessed 07/07/2008).

Oxford Dictionary (2008). *Protestant* [online]. UK: Oxford University Press. Available from: http://www.askoxford.com/concise_oed/protestant?view=uk. (Accessed 19/07/2008).

Page, S.J. (2003). *Tourism Management. Managing for change.* Italy: Genesis Typesetting

Pallister, D. (2003). *Arab boycott of American consumer goods spreads* [online]. UK: The Guardian 08/01/2003. Available from: http://www.guardian.co.uk/world/2003/jan/08/davidpallister. (Accessed 27/07/2008).

Pearson Education (2008). *The Age of Religious Wars* [online]. Available from: http://wps.prenhall.com/hss_kagan_westheritage_8/0,7833,735249-,00.html. Pearson Prentice Hall (Accessed 28/07/2008).

Pelkington, H., Omel'chenko, E., Flynn, M., Bliudina, U. and Starkova, E. (2002). Looking West? Cultural Globalization and Russian Youth Cultures. *Contemporary Sociology.* 32 (6), pp. 730-731.

Perry, M. (2006). *Perceptions of Race in the Arab World* [online]. USA: University of Michigan. Available from: http://inhouse.lau.edu.lb/bima/papers/Perry.pdf. (Accessed 18/07/2008).

Phelps, A. (1986). Holiday destination image – the problems of assessment: An example developed in Menorca. *Tourism Management.* 7 (3), pp. 168-180.

Prebensen, N.K. (2007). Exploring tourists' images of a distant destination. *Tourism Management.* 28 (3), pp.747-756.

Randell-Moon, H. (2006). 'Common Values': Whiteness, Christianity, Asylum Seekers and the Howard Government. *ACRAWSA e-journal.* 2 (1), pp.1-14.

Ratner, C. (2000). A Cultural-Psychological Analysis of Emotions. *Culture and Psychology.* 6, pp.5-39.

Rayappa, V. (2005). *Aligning brands with emerging Arab youth values* [online]. Saudi Arabia: AME Info. Available from: http://www.ameinfo.com/58185.html. (Accessed 18/07/2008).

Redford, K.H. and Brosius, J.B. (2006). Diversity and homogenization in the endgame. *Global Environmental Change.* 16 (4), pp. 317-319.

Reid, D.G. (2003). *Tourism, Globalization And Development: Responsible Tourism Planning.* Sydney: Pluto Press.

Reisinger, Y. and Turner, L.W. (2002a). Cultural Differences between Asian Tourist Markets and Australian Hosts: Part 2. *Journal of Travel Research.* 40 (3), pp.374-384.

Reisinger, Y. and Turner, L.W. (2002b). Cultural Differences between Asian Tourist Markets and Australian Hosts, Part 1. *Journal of Travel Research.* 40 (3), pp.295-315.

Reisinger, Y. and Turner, L.W. (2003). *Cross-Cultural Behaviour in Tourism Concepts and Analysis.* Oxford: Elsevier Science Limited.

Rifkin, J. (2001). *Worlds apart.* UK: The Guardian 03/07/2001. Available from: http://www.guardian.co.uk/world/2001/jul/03/globalisation.comment?commentpage =1 (Accessed 27/07/2008).

Ritzer, G. (2003). The Globalization of Nothing. *SAIS Review.* 23 (2), pp.189-200.

Saeed, A. (2004). *Understanding Egalitarianism in Islam* [online]. New England: The Committee on Racial, Social & Economic Justice. Available from: http://www.neym.org/PrejudiceAndPoverty/Issue12.spring2004.pdf. (Accessed 17/07/2008).

Saunders, M, Lewis, P, Thornhill, A (2003). *Research Methods for Business Students.* Third edition. London: Pearson Education Limited.

Saunders, M, Lewis, P, Thornhill, A (2007). *Research Methods for Business Students.* Fourth edition. London: Pearson Education Limited.

Sbragia, A.M. (2007). *EU Trade Policy and Globalization: Following the American Leader?* [online]. USA: University of Pittsburgh. Available from: http://www.princeton.edu/~smeunier/Sbragia.pdf. (Accessed 15/08/2008).

Schiffman, L.G. and Kanuk, L. (1991). *Consumer Behaviour.* USA: Prentice Hall.

Sharma, S., Shimp, T.A., Shin, J. (1994). Consumer Ethnocentrism: A Test of Antecedents and Moderators. *Journal of the Academy of Marketing Science.* 23 (1), pp.26-37.

Sloan, D. (2008). *How to Compare Data Sets – ANOVA* [online]. USA: iSix Sigma. Available from: http://www.isixsigma.com/library/content/c021111a.asp. (Accessed 12/07/2008).

Smee, J. (2006). *Germany throws out stereotypes with the (very clean) rubbish* [online]. Berlin: Guardian.co.uk. Available from: http://www.guardian.co.uk/world/2006/oct/25/germany.mainsection. (Accessed 12/08/2008).

Smith-Spark, L. (2006). *Can Germany escape its war past?* [online]. UK: BBC, 06/06/2006. Available from: http://news.bbc.co.uk/1/hi/world/europe/5041598.stm. (Accessed 31/07/2008).

Soenmez, S. and Sirakaya, E. (2002). A Distorted Destination Image? The Case of Turkey. *Journal of Travel Research.* 41 (2), pp.185-196.

Spett, M. (2004). *Expressing Negative Emotions: Healthy Catharsis or Sign of Pathology* [online]. Available from: http://www.nj-act.org/article3.html. (Accessed 02/07/2008).

Spiegel (2008). *Deutschland beliebtester Staat – Ansehen der USA waechst erstmals seit Jahren* [online]. Germany: Spiegelonline Politk. Available from: http://www.spiegel.de/politik/ausland/0,1518,544877,00.html. (Accessed 24/06/2008).

Srnka, K., Gegez, A.E. and Arzova, S.B. (2007). Why Is It (Un-)ethical? Comparing Potential European Partners: A Western Christian and An Eastern Islamic Country – On Arguments Used in Explaining Ethical Judgments. *Journal of Business Ethics. 74 (2),* pp. 101-118.

Stabler, M. (1995). The Image of Destination Regions: Theoretical and Empirical Aspects. In: Goodall, B. And Ashworth, G.J. *Marketing in Tourism Industry: The Promotion of Destination Regions.* Ed. Routeledge, pp.133-159.

Stahel, S., Schaer, M. and Zuercher, B. (2008). *Globalisierung: WIE DIE SCHWEIZ GEWINNT* [online]. Switzerland: Avenir Suisse. Available from: http://www.avenir-suisse.ch/en/viewPublication/content/themen/wachstum/leporello-globalisierung.html?publication=1. (Accessed 08/07/2008).

Stengel, M. (2005). *Dolce vita an der Spree: Berlin im Europa-Vergleich spitze* [online]. Berlin: Berliner Morgenpost. Available from: http://www.morgenpost.de/printarchiv/berlin/article354437/Dolce_vita_an_der_Spre e_Berlin_im_Europa_Vergleich_spitze.html. (Accessed 09/08/2008).

Stern, E. and Krakover, S. (1993). The Formation of a Composite Urban Image. *Geographical Analysis.* 25 (2), pp.130-146.

Strohmaier, B. (2006). *Warum die Berliner so freundlich tun* [online]. Germany: Spiegel Online. Available from: https://www.spiegel.de/reise/staedte/0,1518,422723,00.html. (Accessed 12/08/2008).

Sueddeutsche (2007). *Der Preis der Nacht* [online]. Germany: Sueddeutsche.de. Available from: http://www.sueddeutsche.de/reise/artikel/673/133424/. (Accessed 14/08/2008).

Suh, T and Kwon, I.-W.G. (2002). Globalization and reluctant buyers. *International Marketing Review.* 19 (6), pp.663-680.

Sullins, D.P. (1999). Catholic/Protestant Trends on Abortion: Convergence and Polarity. *Journal for the Scientific Study of Religion.* 38 (3), pp.354-369.

Tang, L. and Koveos, P.E. (2008). A framework to update Hofstede's cultural value indices: economic dynamics and institutional stability. *Journal of International Busienss Studies.* pp.1-19.

Tasci, A.D.A (2007). Methodology Influences on Destination Image: The Case of Michigan. *Current Issues in Tourism.* 10 (5), pp. 480-501.

Travel Smart (2008). *Berlin Information and Berlin Tourism (Berlin, Germany)* [online]. Travel Smart Limited: World Guides. Available from: http://www.berlin.world-guides.com/. (Accessed 14/08/2008).

Truong, T.H. and King, B. (2006). Comparing Cross-Cultural Dimensions of the Experiences of International Tourists in Vietnam. *Journal of Business Systems, Governance and Ethics.* 1(1), pp.65-75.

Tucker, S. (2000). *Young people and Youth culture* [online]. Church of Ireland youth department. Available from: www.ciyd.org/moxiecodefiles/uploads/Downloads/youngpeopleculture.doc. (Accessed 28/07/2008).

UNESCO (2006). *Youth Mainstreaming Training Module 1 'Building a Common Vision on Youth* [online]. Cairo: UNESCO. Available from: www.unesco.org/.../Training_in_Cairo_2006/Modules_of_presentation/presentation_1_common_vision.ppt. (Accessed 18/07/2008).

UNWTO (2008a). *Demand remains firm despite uncertainties* [online]. World Tourism Organization. Available from: http://unwto.org/facts/eng/pdf/barometer/UNWTO_Barom08_2_en_Excerpt.pdf. (Accessed 04/07/2008).

UNWTO (2008b). *Youth Travel Matters: Understanding the Global Phenomenon of Youth Travel* [online]. Spain: World Tourism Organization. Available from: http://unwto.org/media/news/en/features_det.php?id=2221&idioma=E. (Accessed 15/07/2008).

US Army (2006). *Arab Cultural Awareness: 58 Factsheets* [online]. Kansas: US Army Training and Doctrine Command. Available from: http://www.fas.org/irp/agency/army/arabculture.pdf. (Accessed 17/07/2008).

Usher, S. (2007). *Arab youth revel in pop revolution* [online]. UK: BBC News. Available from: http://news.bbc.co.uk/1/hi/world/europe/6666725.stm. (Accessed 28/07/2008).

Van Egmond, T. (2005). *Understanding the Tourist Phenomenon: An Analysis of 'West' – 'South' Tourism. Towards Sustainable Tourism Development Strategies for Third World Tourism Destinations.* Proefschrift Wageningen Universiteit.

Veal, A. J. (1997). *Research Methods for Leisure and Tourism, A Practical Guide.* 2nd edition. Great Britain: Financial Times Professional Limited.

Veal, A.J. (2006). *Research Methods for leisure and tourism.* UK: Pearson Education Limited.

Vinson, D.E., Scott, J.E. and Lamont, L.M. (1977). The Role of Personal Values in Marketing and Consumer Behavior. *Journal of Marketing.* 41 (2), pp. 44-50.

Vitale, D.C., Armenakis, A.A. and Field, H.S. (2008). Integrating Qualitative and Quantitative Methods for Organizational Diagnosis. *Journal of Mixed Methods Research.* 2 (1), pp.87-105.

Vogt, C.A. and Andereck, K.L. (2003). Destination Perceptions Across a Vacation. *Journal of Travel Research.* 41, pp.348-354.

Waters, M. (2001). *Globalization.* 2nd edition. London: Routeledge

Weaver, D. And Lawton, C. (2006). *Tourism Management.* 3rd edition. Australia: Wiley.

Wirtz, J. (2001). Book Review: Consumer Behaviour in Asia. *International Marketing Review.* 18 (1), pp.97-102.

Wittlinger, R. (2004). Perceptions of Germany and the Germans in Post-war Britain. *Journal of Multilingual and Multicultural Development.* 25 (5&6), pp. 453-465.

WSV (2006). *Inglehart-Welzel Cultural Map of the World* [online]. Sweden: World Values Survey Association. Available from: http://margaux.grandvinum.se/SebTest/wvs/articles/folder_published/article_base_54 . (Accessed 11/07/2008).

WTTC (2008). *TOURISM LEADERS EXAMINE EMPLOYMENT ISSUE FOR CHINA'S TRAVEL AND TOURISM* [online]. Shanghai, China: World Travel & Tourism Council. Available from: http://www.wttc.org/eng/Tourism_News/Press_Releases/Press_Releases_2008/Touri sm_leaders_examine_employment_issue_for_China%E2%80%99s_Travel__and_To urism/. (Accessed 11/07/2008).

WYSE (2007). *Youth Tourism – The Travel Industry's Boom Sector* [online]. World Youth Student & Educational Travel. Available from: http://www.aboutwysetc.org/Docs/PR_UNWTOPartnership.pdf. (Accessed 15/07/2008).

Zahid, D. (2007). Impact of Cultural Globalization on the Upper Class Youth in Dhaka City: A Sample Study. *Bangladesh e-Journal of Sociology.* 4 (2), pp.1-11.

Zhao, C. (2006). *New Zealand's Destination Image and the Chinese Outbound Market: A comparative study between the Beijing (north) and Guangdong (south) markets.* Thesis (Master). Auckland University of Technology.

Zia-Ebrahimi, R. (2005). *Factors shaping the foreign policy of Saudi Arabia* [online]. Middle East Consultant. Available from: http://www.zia-ebrahimi.com/saudi.html. (Accessed 04/08/2008).

Appendices

Appendix 1

Inglehart - Welzel Cultural Map of the World

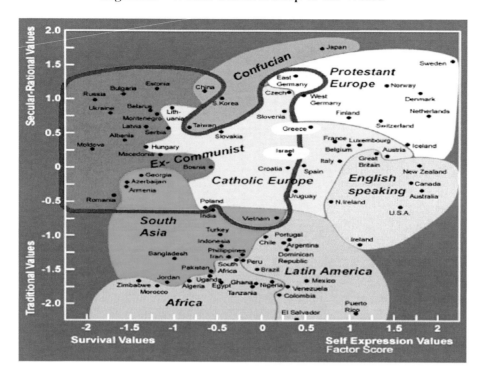

Source: WVS 2006

Appendix 2

The Anholt - GfK Roper Nations Brand Index

The way a country is perceived can make a critical difference to the success of its business, trade and tourism efforts, as well as its diplomatic and cultural relations with other nations. Since 1996, when he coined the term 'nation branding' and gave birth to this important new field, Simon Anholt has been working with governments to help them plan the policies, strategies, investments and innovations which lead their country towards an improved profile and reputation. Anholt developed the Nation Brands IndexSM (NBI) in 2005 as a way to measure the image and reputation of the world's nations, and to track their profiles as they rise or fall.

Now, through a partnership with this renowned government advisor and author, GfK Roper Public Affairs & Media provides an expanded Nation Brands Index, the only analytical ranking of the world's nation brands.

This unique collaboration combines the heritage and authority of GfK Roper's three-quarters of a century of experience in public affairs research with the expertise of Simon Anholt to offer a unique barometer of global opinion. *The Anholt-GfK Roper Nation Brands Index* is a cost-effective and comprehensive system for measuring and managing national reputation around the world. This powerful tool will help you to understand measure and, ultimately, build a strong national image and identity for the government, organizations, regions, and businesses you represent.

Growing from 35 to now 50 countries, *The Anholt-GfK Roper Nation Brands Index* measures the power and quality of each country's 'brand image' by combining the following six dimensions:

- Exports – Determines the public's image of products and services from each country and the extent to which consumers proactively seek or avoid products from each country-of-origin.

- Governance – Measures public opinion regarding the level of national government competency and fairness and describes individuals' beliefs about each country's government, as well as its perceived commitment to global issues such as democracy, justice, poverty and the environment.

- Culture and Heritage – Reveals global perceptions of each nation's heritage and appreciation for its contemporary culture, including film, music, art, sport and literature.

- People – Measures the population's reputation for competence, education, openness and friendliness and other qualities, as well as perceived levels of potential hostility and discrimination.

- Tourism – Captures the level of interest in visiting a country and the draw of natural and man-made tourist attractions.

- Investment and Immigration – Determines the power to attract people to live, work or study in each country and reveals how people perceive a country's economic and social situation.

Appendix 3

CWH & B: European Cities Monitor 20 European Cities most familiar to respondents as a business location

City	Rank			Weighted Score
	1990 +	2004	**2005**	**2005**
London	1	1	**1**	**0.87**
Paris	2	2	**2**	**0.60**
Frankfurt	3	3	**3**	**0.33**
Brussels	4	4	**4**	**0.30**
Barcelona	11	6	**5**	**0.28**
Amsterdam	5	5	**6**	**0.24**
Madrid	17	7	**7**	**0.24**
Berlin	15	9	**8**	**0.19**
Munich	12	8	**9**	**0.18**
Zurich	7	10	**10**	**0.18**
Milan	9	11	**11**	**0.15**
Dublin	-	12	**12**	**0.14**
Prague	23	13	**13**	**0.14**
Lisbon	16	16	**14**	**0.12**
Manchester	13	14	**15**	**0.12**
Düsseldorf	6	18	**16**	**0.10**
Stockholm	19	15	**17**	**0.10**
Geneva	8	17	**18**	**0.10**
Hamburg	14	19	**19**	**0.09**
Warsaw	25	20	**20**	**0.09**

Appendix 4

The Anholt City Brands Index 2005: Berlin's Rank

Overall Rankings	Rank
London	1
Paris	2
Sydney	3
Rome	4
Barcelona	5
Amsterdam	6
New York	7
Los Angeles	8
Madrid	9
Berlin	10
San Francisco	11
Toronto	12
Geneva	13
Washington	14
Brussels	15
Milan	16
Stockholm	17
Edinburgh	18
Tokyo	19
Prague	20
Hong Kong	21
Singapore	22
Rio de Janeiro	23
Beijing	24
Mexico City	25
Moscow	26
Johannesburg	27
Cairo	28
Mumbai	29
Lagos	30

Appendix 5

Globalisation & World cities Group (GAWC)

A. ALPHA WORLD CITIES
12: London, Paris, New York, Tokyo
10: Chicago, Frankfurt, Hong Kong, Los Angeles, Milan, Singapore
----
B. BETA WORLD CITIES
9: San Francisco, Sydney, Toronto, Zurich
8: Brussels, Madrid, Mexico City, Sao Paulo
7: Moscow, Seoul

C. GAMMA WORLD CITIES
6: Amsterdam, Boston, Caracas, Dallas, Dusseldorf, Geneva, Houston, Jakarta, Johannesburg, Melbourne, Osaka, Prague, Santiago, Taipei, Washington
5: Bangkok, Beijing, Rome, Stockholm, Warsaw
4: Atlanta, Barcelona, Berlin, Buenos Aires, Budapest, Copenhagen, Hamburg, Istanbul, Kuala Lumpur, Manila, Miami, Minneapolis, Montreal, Munich, Shanghai

Appendix 6

Questionnaire in English

Berlin's Image as a tourist destination

This survey is conducted on behalf of Bournemouth University and is part of a research project. The outcome of the questionnaire will help us to identify relevant cross-cultural differences or similarities in the perception of Germany's capital Berlin, as a tourist destination. This questionnaire is not about what you know of the city of Berlin, but about what you think or how you perceive Berlin. Even if you have never visited Berlin, you might have consciously or unconsciously formed a certain image of Germany's metropolis. The outcome will only be used for general statistics and will be treated confidential. It would be highly appreciated if you could spare 5 minutes of your valuable time to fill in the questionnaire. Thank you in expectation.

1) Some demographics of you
    a) Age: 15-18 [ ] 19-25 [ ] older [ ] b) Gender: Male [ ] Female [ ]
    c) Cultural background: Arabic [ ] British [ ] other [ ] _____   d) Country of residence: _____
    e) Education: High School or less [ ] Some university [ ]   University [ ] Master or PhD [ ]

2) Have you ever been to Berlin?   Yes [] No []

3) What comes first to your mind, when you think about Berlin? (Please tick only one)
    History [ ] Nightlife & Entertainment [ ] Political Centre [ ] Cultural Attractions [ ]
    Shopping facilities [ ] Architectural Attractions [ ] Capital [ ]

4) Functional Attributes: Do you agree with the following statements on what Berlin has to offer?

	Strongly agree	Agree	Undecided	Disagree	Strongly Disagree
Fair prices					
Good Infrastructure					
Easy accessibility					
Rich gastronomy					
Good quality of accommodation					
Good shopping facilities					

Rich cultural offer					
Brilliant nightlife					
Interesting historical sights					
Various parks/Nature					

5) Psychological Attributes: Do the following attributes match your own image of Berlin?

	Strongly agree	Agree	Undecided	Disagree	Strongly Disagree
Friendly people					
Generally safe					
Clean					
Young					
Fun/enjoyable					

6) Functional Holistic: Do you view Berlin as, …

	Strongly agree	Agree	Undecided	Disagree	Strongly Disagree
Vivid cityscape					
Green					
Multi-cultural					
Well-groomed					
Noble/classy					
Beautiful					
Tolerant					
Modern					

7) Psychological Holistic: Imagine you are visiting Berlin. How do you think, would you experience the city of Berlin?

	Strongly agree	Agree	Undecided	Disagree	Strongly Disagree
Pleasant					
Lively/dynamic					
Exciting					
Entertaining					
Attractive/Interesting					
Charming					
Trendy/Cool					
Creative/Innovative					
Good atmosphere for					

tourists					

8) How do you rate your overall image of Berlin as a tourist destination?
Very Positive [ ] Positive [ ] Neutral [ ] Negative [ ] Very Negative

Thank you for your participation.

Questionnaire in German

Berlins Image als Tourismusstandort

Sehr geehrte Damen und Herren,
ich heiße Wassim El Kadhi und bin Masterstudent an der Bournemouth Universität in Großbritannien. Derzeit schreibe ich an meiner Diplomarbeit, welche das Image Berlins als Tourismusstandort in Großbritannien und den arabischen Ländern untersucht. Um eine aussagekräftige und relevante Studie zusammenstellen zu können, bitte ich Sie sich 5 Minuten Ihrer wertvollen Zeit zu nehmen, um diesen Fragebogen auszufüllen. Auch wenn Sie noch nie in Berlin waren, werden Sie ein bestimmtes Bild von Berlin haben. Bei diesem Fragebogen geht es nicht darum herauszufinden, was Sie über Berlin wissen, nein, es geht darum herauszufinden, was Sie von Berlin denken und was für ein Bild Sie von der Stadt haben. Ihre Antworten werden vertraulich behandelt und tragen möglicherweise zu wissenschaftlichen Fortschritten bei. Ich bedanke mich im Voraus für Ihre Teilnahme an dieser Umfrage.

1) Demographische Angaben
   a) Alter: 15-18 [ ] 19-25 [ ] älter [ ] b) Geschlecht: Männlich [ ] Weiblich [ ]
   c) Ethnischer Hintergrund: arabisch [ ] britisch [ ] sonstige [ ] _____ d) Land
   ihres Wohnorts: _____
   e) Ausbildung: Gymnasium oder weniger [ ]   Universität [ ] Diplom oder
   Doktor [ ]

2) Waren Sie schon mal in Berlin?   Ja [] Nein []

3) Was kommt Ihnen als erstes in den Sinn, wenn Sie an Berlin denken? (Bitte nur eine Antwortmöglichkeit ankreuzen)
   Geschichte [ ] Nachtleben & Unterhaltung [ ] Politisches Zentrum [ ] Kulturelle Sehenswürdigkeiten [ ] Shoppingmöglichkeiten [ ] Architektonische Sehenswürdigkeiten [ ] Hauptstadt [ ]

4) Stimmen Sie den folgenden Zitaten über das touristische Angebot Berlins zu?

	Stimme entschieden zu	Stimme zu	Neutral	Stimme nicht zu	Stimme ganz und gar nicht zu
Gutes Preis-leistungs-Niveau					
Gute Infrastruktur					
Leichte Erreichbarkeit (zum Beispiel per Flugzeug)					
Breites gastronomisches Angebot					
Hervorragende Unterkünfte					
Gute Shoppingmöglichkeiten					
Reiches Kulturangebot					
Lebendiges Nachtleben					
Interessante historische Sehenswürdigkeiten					
Viele Parks/Natur					

5) Passen die folgenden Attribute zu deinem eigenen Berlin-Bild?

	Stimme entschieden zu	Stimme zu	Neutral	Stimme nicht zu	Stimme ganz und gar nicht zu
Freundliche Menschen					
Im allgemeinen sicher					
Sauber					
Junge Stadt					
Spaß/Amüsant					

6) Sehen Sie Berlin als,…

	Stimme entschieden zu	Stimme zu	Neutral	Stimme nicht zu	Stimme ganz und gar nicht zu
Lebendige Stadt					
Grün/Naturbewusst					
Multi-kulturell					
Gepflegt					
Nobel					
Schoen					
Tolerant					
Modern					

7) Stellen Sie sich vor, Sie besuchten gerade Berlin. Was glauben Sie, wie Sie die Stadt Berlin wahrnehmen würden?

	Stimme entschieden zu	Stimme zu	Neutral	Stimme nicht zu	Stimme ganz und gar nicht zu
Sympathisch/Angenehm					
Lebendig/Dynamisch					
Aufregend					
Unterhaltsam					
Attraktiv/Interessant					
Charmant					
Trendig/Cool					
Kreativ/Innovativ					
Gute Atmosphäre für Touristen					

8) Wie schätzt du dein allgemeines Image/Bild von Berlin als Tourismusstandort ein?

Sehr positiv[ ] Positiv [ ] Neutral [ ] Negativ [ ] Sehr Negativ

Danke für Ihre Teilnahme an der Umfrage!!!

صورة برلين كمدينة سياحية

سيداتي، سادتي الأفاضل،

أنا المسمى وسيم القاضي طالب ومتحصل على شهادة الأستاذية بجامعة _Bournemouth_ ببريطانيا العظمى أنا الآن بصدد الإعداد مذكرة حول صورة برلين كمدينة سياحية في بريطانيا العظمى والدول العربية من أجل إعداد دراسة واضحة ودقيقة أرجو منكم تخصيص 5 دقائق من وقتكم من أجل الإجابة على الأسئلة التالية، أيضا إن كنت لم تذهب إلى برلين من قبل، من المؤكد أن لك صورة عن برلين هذا الاستجواب ليس موجها لمعرفة معلوماتك عن برلين بل هو موجه لمعرفة رأيك وتصورك لبرلين سيقع دراسة إجابتك في كنف السرية وربما تساهم هذه الإجابات في تحقيق بعض التقدم العلمي.

أشكرك مسبقا عن مساهمتك في هذا البحث.

1) <u>المعطيات الديمغرافية :</u>

- <u>العمر :</u>
  - o من 15 سنة إلى 18 سنة ☐
  - o من 19 سنة إلى 25 سنة ☐
  - o أكبر من 25 سنة ☐

الجنس :

- ○ ذكر ☐
- ○ أنثى ☐

الجنسية :

- ○ عربية ☐
- ○ بريطانية ☐
- ○ أخرى ☐

- • بلد الإقامة : ....

- • المستوى التعليمي :

- ○ إعدادي ☐
- ○ ثانوي ☐

- ○ جامعي ☐
- ○ أخرى ☐

2) هل زرت برلين من قبل ؟

نعم ☐   لا ☐

3) ما هو أول ما يأتي إلى مخيلتكم عندما تفكرون في برلين (الرجاء اختيار إجابة واحدة).

- ○ تاريخها ☐

- ○ الحياة الليلية والترفيه ☐
- ○ مركز سياسي ☐
- ○ معالم ثقافية ☐
- ○ إمكانيات التسوق المتعددة ☐
- ○ معالم هندسية ☐
- ○ عاصمة ☐

4) هل تساندون الأقوال التالية المتعلقة بالسياحة في برلين

	أعارض بشدة	أعارض	محايد	أوافق	أوافق بشدة
الأسعار مستوى المعيشة جيدان					
بنية تحتية جيدة					
سهولة الوصول (مثلا طائرة)					
توفر عدة أنواع من المطاعم (إيطالية، فرنسية تونسية...)					
سكن رائع					
سهولة التسوق					
ثقافة ثرية					
حياة ليلية متوفرة					
معالم تاريخية مثيرة للاهتمام					

					منتزهات ومناطق خضراء كثيرة

5) أجب حسب نظرتك الشخصية :

أعارض بشدة	أعارض	محايد	أوافق	أوافق بشدة	
					أشخاص متفتحون
					آمنة إجمالا
					نظيفة
					مدينة شابة
					ممتعة مرفهة

6) ترون برلين كمدينة :

أعارض بشدة	أعارض	محايد	أوافق	أوافق بشدة	
					دائمة الحركة
					خضراء
					متعددة الثقافات
					دائمة الصيانة
					نبيلة
					جميلة
					متفتحة
					عصرية

7) تصور أنك في برلين كيف تتخيل نظرتك لها :

أعارض بشدة	أعارض	محايد	أوافق	أوافق بشدة	
					لطيفة
					حية دائمة الحركة
					مثيرة
					مسلية
					جذابة
					ساحرة
					عصرية
					مبدعة مجددة
					جو جميل للسياحة

8) كيف هي نظرتك العامة لبرلين؟

إيجابية جدا ☐   إيجابية ☐   محايدة ☐   سلبية ☐   سلبية جدا ☐

شكرا لمشاركتك في الاستجواب

142

Focus group interviews at EF School, Bournemouth

1st Interview	2nd Interview	3rd Interview	4th Interview	5th Interview
9 students →	8 students →	3 students →	3 students →	2 students →
				1 Norway (F, 25)
2 Saudi-Arabia (M, 23&19)	1 Sweden (M,23)	2 Norway (F, 17&16)	1 Switzerland (M, 17)	1 Switzerland (F, 19)
1 Jordan (M, 24)	1 Norway (F, 21)	1 Denmark (F, 18)	2 Spain (F, 19&21)	
1 Kuwait (M, 21)	1 UK (F, 25)			**6th Interview**
1 British (F, 24, teacher)	1 Netherlands (F, 23)			
Rest from Asia	Rest from Eastern Europe & France			1 teacher → UK (F, 24)

Interview example

Introduction:

The first group discussion was conducted with a class of nine students. The teacher was considered as a student too, since she was 24 years old. See above for details of the interviewees. Asians' contribution to the group discussion was not considered during the analysis of the results. Before the interview was started each of the participants was asked for their name and country of origin and whether they had already been to Berlin. Then they were introduced to the topic and were given questionnaires, so that they could refer to it when required, since they were language students, with difficulties to come up with appropriate adjectives.

Start of the interview

The researcher: When you refer to question 3 on the questionnaire. What comes first into your mind when you think of Berlin as a tourist destination?

Shelley, 24, Bournemouth (UK): *'Nightlife and Entertainment comes to my mind first. I have never been to Berlin, but I have been told a lot about it.'*

Mubarek, 23, Jeddah (Saudi Arabia): *'Cold war, the Berlin wall and history'*

Hamsa, 21, from Kuwait: *'Just capital'*

The researcher: Imagine you would be in Berlin right now. What kind of atmosphere or mood would you expect to find in Berlin? (They could not really come up with anything by themselves, did not have a clear picture of Berlin).

Shelley: *'Cosmopolitan I would think'*

Hamsa: *'I think dynamic...I am not planning to go there'*

The researcher: Could you furthermore think about unique tourist attractions in Berlin? (Limited responses, picture still unclear)

Fares, 19, Saudi-Arabia: *'War tanks and the wall'*

Youssef, 24, Jordan: *'Architectural attractions related to Second World War come into his mind'*

The researcher: How would you expect people to be in Berlin?

Fares: *'I think they are a bit arrogant'*

Mubarek:: *'Unfriendly, cause I have this image about Germany they are not friendly'*

Hamsa: *'They don't like to speak English'*

Mubarek: *'I have this impression about them, but I am not sure'*

The researcher: So if you think about Berlin do you rather think about Germany on the whole or about Berlin in particular?

Mubarek: *'No about Germany'*

The researcher: Shelley can I ask you again what do you think about Germans?

Shelley: '*I was just thinking about this. I know the whole country and I know including Berlin has probably a lot of immigration now. But I have a lot of German friends and quite a lot of them from Berlin and I find the quite from the point of view of a British person; I find them quite narrow-minded. And I would be quite interested to know, you know, what it is like for an immigrant in Berlin. I would think it'd be a little bit difficult for tourists to be there. And consequently, it must be difficult for a tourist to be there. But again this is just going by a few or one or two, the attitudes of one or two Germans that I often have arguments with.*'

The researcher: For the girls. Imagine Berlin was a man. How would you imagine this man to look like?

Patricia, 17, Norway: '*Tall, blond, white, green eyes*'

The researcher: For the guys. Imagine Berlin was a girl. How would you imagine this girl to look like?

Hamsa: '*Same as man I think tall and blond*'

.

Mubarek: '*Tall and big....green eyes and they are beautiful. And also they are beautiful*'

Hamsa: '*No, they are not, they are ugly*'

Mubarek:' *I know one Germany girl, she is beautiful*'.

The researcher: How do you think about Berlin's physical appearance?

Mubarek: '*Very European*'

Fares: '*Very European. Historical buildings...old buildings.*'

Shelley, 24: '*Half of it must look very communist....Russian style*'

Hamsa: '*I think is combination there is old town maybe with a old building and modern one*'

Mubarek:' *I think it's green city because it is in Europe...we have an image of Europe being not like our countries....and very good infrastructure because it is in Europe*'

The researcher: A particular question to my Arab friends. Could you please mention three European cities that you would like to visit?

Fares: '*Stockholm, Paris and Berlin*'.

Youssef: '*Dublin, maybe Berlin and Milan*'

Mubarek: '*Vienna and...Amsterdam and Geneva*'
Hamsa: '*Cannes, Spain and Italy*'

The researcher. Again for the Arabs. How would you rate Berlin's accessibility from Arab countries?

Mubarek: '*The most important thing the language...If you go to Switzerland, Spain they would like to speak with you in English. I'm not sure if I'm right or not but in Germany they don't like to speak. So you find problems at times you need to bring one to translate*'.

The researcher: So you think that Germany is not really accessible because of the language and because of unfriendly people?

Fares: '*We heard about the English men, but when we came here, the image changed*'.

Mubarek: '*One of my friends' works for Saudian business in Berlin, so he told me that and I'm planning to visit him, <u>not for Berlin</u>, but to visit my friend*'.

Hamsa: *'I think Germany in health-care tourism is famous in Kuwait, in my country.For health-care tourism'.*

Mubarek: *'Health care yes. All Saudis go to Germany for medical tourism and to buy Mercedes. To buy cars.'*

What information sources have mostly formed your image of Berlin?

Shelley: *'Friends'*

Fares: 'Internet'

Mubarek: *'Word of mouth*

Hamsa: *'Internet, TV like education, documentaries'*

The researcher:Maybe school. Do you have history classes about Germany and Berlin in general?

Hamsa: *'No'.*

The researcher: **What is your overall image of Berlin?**

Shelley: *'Rather negative, it's not a place that I would visit... But then you know if it comes to European countries I think Germany is the last on my list that I would consider to visit'. '*

The researcher: That is the attitude of British towards Germany.

Shelley*: 'Yes. You were saying about television the coverage of television in the historical after the World War 2, we get a lot of that on British TV. Hmm you love sort of hearing of World War 2.'*

Fares: *'Positive'*

Youssef: *'Neutral.'*

Mubarek: *'Neutral'*

Hamsa: *'Negative. I like activities, especially water activities, so my hobby is down in the Mediterranean not in the cold places'.*

The researcher: Thank you very much for your attention

A few written comments on Berlin after the focus group discussions

1) Female, 21, Norway

''Berlin is a modern city with a lively nightlife, cultural life and good cuisine. I guess it is popular for tourists. And not very expensive''.

2) Male, 23, Sweden

''Berlin is cosmopolitan and has changed a lot. I think it is modern, but still with a lot of history. It must be an attractive place''.

3) Male, 23, Saudi Arabia

''Berlin is a big city, high buildings and cold. Not really sunny with serious and organized people.''

4) Male, 19, Saudi Arabia

''The houses are very well organized, the gardens of people very well tidied. Good looking city.''

5) Male, 21, Kuwait

''Berlin is a cold and cosmopolitan city with lots of parks''

Comments on Berlin via e-mail

1) Male, 24, Jordan

''When I try to visualise Berlin, I can see a remarkable combination of the old and the modern. Sadly, I can't give any examples: the Berlin Wall is the only thing that springs to mind. A lot of beer...traditional music & outfits...But I imagine it as a neat, clean, organised city.''

2) Female, 24, Jordan

''I hope you received good information for your work. When you ask me, I think or I imagine Berlin like an interesting place for people that interested in history or sociology, because there they can remember what happened during the war. I heard from friends that many foreigners in Berlin, but also strong racial segregation and ethnic groupings which is a consequence from the war. Overall I am not attracted by Berlin''

3) Female, 21, Egypt

''Hi Wassim. Maybe it's too late but I think of Berlin that it is a very big city with many old and many new buildings. I would think that I would meet people from everywhere in the world there because it is the capital of Germany. I think you can make a lot there, but to be honest I don't know more.''

4) Female, 23, Egypt

'Berlin must be beautiful in the summer very green and organized. Also with a lot of nice buildings'

5) Female, 18, Denmark

''Berlin is a big cosmopolitan city, adapted to new ways of life and technical development. It is full of history and multi-cultural with lots of possibilities for work and study. Lots of young people drinking beer around Brandenburg Door and a lot of tourists buying pieces of the Berlin Wall and looking forward to see the holocaust.''

6) Female, 25, Denmark

''I think of Berlin as a tourist destination that it is very safe and a pleasant capital. I imagine Berlin to be a huge metropolis. Compared to other German places, Berlin must be very active and lively and has many historical sites and very good infrastructure. I think also that tourist can see a lot in Berlin and that it is really multi-cultural.''

7) Male, 25, Netherlands

''Based on information from the media and friends I have the following picture of Berlin: Berlin is an open-minded and cosmopolitan city and has a varied scene, because of this I know that Berlin is very popular among young people. Berlin is also very liberal and has a homosexual mayor. I know he always says ''und das ist gut so''. In some parts of Berlin most people speak Turkish but I never hear about any conflicts or so because of this. I really think Berlin is liberal and doesn't only pretend to be so. Berlin is simply a cosmopolitan city. Maybe they are because during the Cold War Berlin experienced things that were much worse. I know some people from Berlin and I consider Berliners to be quite easy-going and funny. I think Berlin must be a crazy place, but still very calm.''

8) Female, 19, Switzerland

''Berlin is a modern city with a lot of attractions. There are lots of tourists everywhere. People drink beer and eat sausages in bars & cafes.''

Appendix 8

Pilot questionnaire

<u>Berlin's Image as a tourist destination</u>

1) Some demographics of you
a) Age: 15-18 [ ] 19-25 [ ] older [ ] b) Gender: Male [ ] Female [ ]   c) Cultural background: Arabic [ ] British [ ] other [ ] _____

2) Have you ever been to Berlin?   Yes [] No []

3) What comes first to your mind, when you think about Berlin?
History [ ] Nightlife & Entertainment [ ] Political Centre [ ] Cultural Attractions [ ] Shopping facilities [ ] Architectural Attractions [ ] Capital [ ]

4) Functional Attributes: Do you agree with the following statements on what Berlin has to offer?

	Strongly agree	Agree	Undecided	Disagree	Strongly Disagree
Fair prices					

150

Good Infrastructure					
Easy accessibility					
Rich gastronomy					
Good quality of accommodation					
Good shopping facilities					
Rich cultural offer					
Brilliant nightlife					
Interesting historical sights					
Various parks/Nature					

5) Psychological Attributes: Do the following attributes match your own image of Berlin?

	Strongly agree	Agree	Undecided	Disagree	Strongly Disagree
Friendly people					
Generally safe					
Clean					
Young					
Fun/enjoyable					

6) Functional Holistic: Do you view Berlin as, …

	Strongly agree	Agree	Undecided	Disagree	Strongly Disagree
Vivid cityscape					
Green					
Multi-cultural					
Well-groomed					
Noble/classy					
Beautiful					
Tolerant					
Modern					

7) Psychological Holistic: Imagine you are visiting Berlin. What kind of feeling, do you think, would you develop of the city of Berlin?

	Strongly agree	Agree	Undecided	Disagree	Strongly Disagree
Pleasant					

Lively/dynamic					
Exciting					
Entertaining					
Attractive/Interesting					
Charming					
Trendy/Cool					
Creative/Innovative					
Good atmosphere for tourists					

8) How do you rate your overall image of Berlin as a tourist destination? Very Positive [ ] Positive [ ] Neutral [ ] Negative [ ] Very Negative

Thank you for your participation.

Appendix 9

ANOVA explained

In 1920, Sir Ronald A. Fisher invented a statistical way to compare data sets. Fisher called his method the Analysis of Variance, which was later dubbed an ANOVA. This method eventually evolved into Six Sigma data set comparisons. An ANOVA is a guide for determining whether or not an event was most likely due to the random chance of natural variation. Or, conversely, the same method provides guidance in saying with a 95% level of confidence that a certain factor (X) or factors (X, Y, and/or Z) were the more likely reason for the event.

The F ratio is the probability information produced by an ANOVA. It was named for Fisher. The orthogonal array and the Results Project, DMAIC designed experiment's cube were also his inventions.

An ANOVA can be, and ought to be, used to evaluate differences between data sets. It can be used with any number of data sets, recorded from any process. The data sets need not be equal in size. Data sets suitable for an ANOVA can be as small as three or four numbers, to infinitely large sets of numbers.

Source: Sloan 2008

Appendix 10

Detailed SPSS results for question 1

Age group

		Frequency	Percent	Valid Percent	Cumulative Percent
Valid	15-18	33	13.8	13.8	13.8
	19-25	206	86.2	86.2	100.0
	Total	239	100.0	100.0	

Gender

		Frequency	Percent	Valid Percent	Cumulative Percent
Valid	female	135	56.5	56.5	56.5
	male	104	43.5	43.5	100.0
	Total	239	100.0	100.0	

Cultural background

		Frequency	Percent	Valid Percent	Cumulative Percent
Valid	Arab-Islamic	103	43.1	43.1	43.1
	Protestant European	136	56.9	56.9	100.0
	Total	239	100.0	100.0	

Country of origin

		Frequency	Percent	Valid Percent	Cumulative Percent
Valid	UK	25	10.5	10.5	10.5
	Netherlands	48	20.1	20.1	30.5
	Germany	20	8.4	8.4	38.9
	Norway	16	6.7	6.7	45.6

		Frequency	Percent	Valid Percent	Cumulative Percent
	Denmark	15	6.3	6.3	51.9
	Sweden	12	5.0	5.0	56.9
	UAE	24	10.0	10.0	66.9
	Egypt	20	8.4	8.4	75.3
	Jordan	23	9.6	9.6	84.9
	Qatar	12	5.0	5.0	90.0
	Saudi Arabia	24	10.0	10.0	100.0
	Total	239	100.0	100.0	

Education

		Frequency	Percent	Valid Percent	Cumulative Percent
Valid	High School or less	43	18.0	18.1	18.1
	Some university	51	21.3	21.4	39.5
	University	100	41.8	42.0	81.5
	Master or PhD	44	18.4	18.5	100.0
	Total	238	99.6	100.0	
Missing	System	1	.4		
Total		239	100.0		

Gender * Cultural background Crosstabulation

			Cultural background		Total
			Arab-Islamic	Protestant European	
Gender	female	Count	42	93	135
		% within Gender	31.1%	68.9%	100.0%
		% within Cultural background	40.8%	68.4%	56.5%
	male	Count	61	43	104
		% within Gender	58.7%	41.3%	100.0%
		% within Cultural background	59.2%	31.6%	43.5%
Total		Count	103	136	239
		% within Gender	43.1%	56.9%	100.0%

Gender * Cultural background Crosstabulation

			Cultural background		
			Arab-Islamic	Protestant European	Total
female	Count		42	93	135
	% within Gender		31.1%	68.9%	100.0%
	% within Cultural background		40.8%	68.4%	56.5%
male	Count		61	43	104
	% within Gender		58.7%	41.3%	100.0%
	% within Cultural background		59.2%	31.6%	43.5%
	Count		103	136	239
	% within Gender		43.1%	56.9%	100.0%
	% within Cultural background		100.0%	100.0%	100.0%

Age group * Cultural background Crosstabulation

			Cultural background		
			Arab-Islamic	Protestant European	Total
Age group	15-18	Count	8	25	33
		% within Age group	24.2%	75.8%	100.0%
		% within Cultural background	7.8%	18.4%	13.8%
	19-25	Count	95	111	206
		% within Age group	46.1%	53.9%	100.0%
		% within Cultural background	92.2%	81.6%	86.2%
	Total	Count	103	136	239
		% within Age group	43.1%	56.9%	100.0%
		% within Cultural background	100.0%	100.0%	100.0%

Country of origin * Cultural background Crosstabulation

	Cultural background

			Arab-Islamic	Protestant European	Total
Country of origin	UK	Count	0	25	25
		% within Country of origin	.0%	100.0%	100.0%
		% within Cultural background	.0%	18.4%	10.5%
	Netherlands	Count	0	48	48
		% within Country of origin	.0%	100.0%	100.0%
		% within Cultural background	.0%	35.3%	20.1%
	Germany	Count	0	20	20
		% within Country of origin	.0%	100.0%	100.0%
		% within Cultural background	.0%	14.7%	8.4%
	Norway	Count	0	16	16
		% within Country of origin	.0%	100.0%	100.0%
		% within Cultural background	.0%	11.8%	6.7%
	Denmark	Count	0	15	15
		% within Country of origin	.0%	100.0%	100.0%
		% within Cultural background	.0%	11.0%	6.3%
	Sweden	Count	0	12	12
		% within Country of origin	.0%	100.0%	100.0%
		% within Cultural background	.0%	8.8%	5.0%
	UAE	Count	24	0	24
		% within Country of origin	100.0%	.0%	100.0%
		% within Cultural background	23.3%	.0%	10.0%
	Egypt	Count	20	0	20

			100.0%	.0%	100.0%
		% within Country of origin			
		% within Cultural background	19.4%	.0%	8.4%
	Jordan	Count	23	0	23
		% within Country of origin	100.0%	.0%	100.0%
		% within Cultural background	22.3%	.0%	9.6%
	Qatar	Count	12	0	12
		% within Country of origin	100.0%	.0%	100.0%
		% within Cultural background	11.7%	.0%	5.0%
	Saudi Arabia	Count	24	0	24
		% within Country of origin	100.0%	.0%	100.0%
		% within Cultural background	23.3%	.0%	10.0%
	Total	Count	103	136	239
		% within Country of origin	43.1%	56.9%	100.0%
		% within Cultural background	100.0%	100.0%	100.0%

Appendix 11

Detailed SPSS results for question 3

What comes first to your mind, when thinking about Berlin?

		Frequency	Percent	Valid Percent	Cumulative Percent
Valid	History	104	43.5	43.7	43.7
	Nightlife&Entertainment	17	7.1	7.1	50.8
	Political Centre	19	7.9	8.0	58.8
	Cultural attractions	22	9.2	9.2	68.1
	Shopping facilities	4	1.7	1.7	69.7

	Architectural attractions	15	6.3	6.3	76.1
	Capital	57	23.8	23.9	100.0
	Total	238	99.6	100.0	
Missing	System	1	.4		
Total		239	100.0		

What comes first to your mind, when thinking about Berlin? * Cultural background Crosstabulation

			Cultural background	
			Arab-Islamic	Protestant European
What comes first to your mind, when thinking about Berlin?	History	Count	45	59
		% within What comes first to your mind, when thinking about Berlin?	43.3%	56.7%
		% within Cultural background	43.7%	43.7%
		% of Total	18.9%	24.8%
	Nightlife&Entertainment	Count	11	6
		% within What comes first to your mind, when thinking about Berlin?	64.7%	35.3%
		% within Cultural background	10.7%	4.4%
		% of Total	4.6%	2.5%
	Political Centre	Count	9	10
		% within What comes first to your mind, when	47.4%	52.6%

		thinking about Berlin?		
	Cultural attractions	% within Cultural background	8.7%	7.4%
		% of Total	3.8%	4.2%
		Count	9	13
		% within What comes first to your mind, when thinking about Berlin?	40.9%	59.1%
	Shopping facilities	% within Cultural background	8.7%	9.6%
		% of Total	3.8%	5.5%
		Count	1	3
		% within What comes first to your mind, when thinking about Berlin?	25.0%	75.0%
	Architectural attractions	% within Cultural background	1.0%	2.2%
		% of Total	.4%	1.3%
		Count	5	10
		% within What comes first to your mind, when thinking about Berlin?	33.3%	66.7%
	Capital	% within Cultural background	4.9%	7.4%
		% of Total	2.1%	4.2%
		Count	23	34
		% within What comes first to your mind, when thinking about Berlin?	40.4%	59.6%
		% within Cultural background	22.3%	25.2%
		% of Total	9.7%	14.3%
Total		Count	103	135

	% within What comes first to your mind, when thinking about Berlin?	43.3%	56.7%
	% within Cultural background	100.0%	100.0%
	% of Total	43.3%	56.7%

What comes first to your mind, when thinking of Berlin?

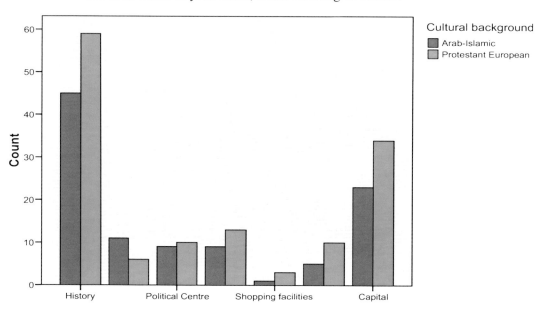

Appendix 12

Detailed SPSS results for question 4
Descriptives

		N	Mean	Std. Deviation
Fair prices	Arab-Islamic	102	2.88	.882
	Protestant European	136	2.51	.789
	Total	238	2.67	.848
Good Infrastructure	Arab-Islamic	103	2.04	.713
	Protestant European	136	1.95	.681

	Total	239	1.99	.695
Easy accessibility	Arab-Islamic	103	2.36	.827
	Protestant European	136	1.96	.614
	Total	239	2.13	.738
Rich gastronomy	Arab-Islamic	103	2.87	.974
	Protestant European	136	2.49	.911
	Total	239	2.66	.987
Good quality of accommodation	Arab-Islamic	100	2.17	.842
	Protestant European	136	2.21	.634
	Total	236	2.19	.728
Good shopping facilities	Arab-Islamic	101	2.05	.853
	Protestant European	136	2.02	.725
	Total	237	2.03	.780
Rich cultural offer	Arab-Islamic	103	1.90	.735
	Protestant European	136	1.85	.821
	Total	239	1.87	.784
Brilliant nightlife	Arab-Islamic	101	2.45	.932
	Protestant European	136	2.20	.850
	Total	237	2.30	.893
Interesting historical sights	Arab-Islamic	103	1.90	.721
	Protestant European	136	1.63	.686
	Total	239	1.75	.713
Various parks/nature	Arab-Islamic	103	2.27	.910
	Protestant European	135	2.59	.892
	Total	238	2.45	.912

ANOVA for Functional Attributes

		Sum of Squares	df	F	Sig.
Fair prices	Between Groups	7.878	1	11.437	.001
	Within Groups	162.559	236		

	Total	170.437	237		
Good Infrastructure	Between Groups	.478	1	.989	.321
	Within Groups	114.484	237		
	Total	114.962	238		
Easy accessibility	Between Groups	9.191	1	18.072	.000
	Within Groups	120.525	237		
	Total	129.715	238		
Rich gastronomy	Between Groups	8.514	1	9.035	.003
	Within Groups	223.352	237		
	Total	231.866	238		
Good quality of accommodation	Between Groups	.074	1	.140	.709
	Within Groups	124.345	234		
	Total	124.419	235		
Good shopping facilities	Between Groups	.044	1	.071	.790
	Within Groups	143.686	235		
	Total	143.730	236		
Rich cultural offer	Between Groups	.146	1	.237	.627
	Within Groups	146.088	237		
	Total	146.234	238		
Brilliant nightlife	Between Groups	3.536	1	4.502	.035
	Within Groups	184.590	235		
	Total	188.127	236		
Interesting historical sights	Between Groups	4.290	1	8.717	.003
	Within Groups	116.647	237		
	Total	120.937	238		
Various parks/nature	Between Groups	6.011	1	7.428	.007
	Within Groups	190.981	236		
	Total	196.992	237		

Level of Agreement in Mean Values for each attribute by Nationality

Descriptives

		N	Mean	Std. Deviation
Fair prices	UK	25	2.64	.952

	Netherlands	48	2.65	.838
	Germany	20	2.45	.759
	Norway	16	2.38	.619
	Denmark	15	2.13	.516
	Sweden	12	2.50	.674
	UAE	24	2.88	.900
	Egypt	20	2.80	1.005
	Jordan	23	2.83	.937
	Qatar	12	2.75	.866
	Saudi Arabia	23	3.09	.733
	Total	238	2.67	.848
Good Infrastructure	UK	25	1.92	.702
	Netherlands	48	2.08	.710
	Germany	20	1.90	.718
	Norway	16	1.81	.750
	Denmark	15	1.93	.458
	Sweden	12	1.75	.622
	UAE	24	2.00	.722
	Egypt	20	1.75	.639
	Jordan	23	2.26	.689
	Qatar	12	2.00	.603
	Saudi Arabia	24	2.13	.797
	Total	239	1.99	.695
Easy accessibility	UK	25	2.08	.640
	Netherlands	48	1.96	.544
	Germany	20	1.95	.759
	Norway	16	1.94	.574
	Denmark	15	2.07	.704
	Sweden	12	1.67	.492
	UAE	24	2.13	.947
	Egypt	20	2.30	.657
	Jordan	23	2.43	.896
	Qatar	12	2.25	.754
	Saudi Arabia	24	2.63	.770
	Total	239	2.13	.738
Rich gastronomy	UK	25	2.72	.891
	Netherlands	48	2.75	.812
	Germany	20	2.10	1.021
	Norway	16	2.25	.856
	Denmark	15	2.00	.756
	Sweden	12	2.58	.996
	UAE	24	2.67	1.090

	Egypt	20	2.75	1.118
	Jordan	23	3.26	1.010
	Qatar	12	3.08	1.165
	Saudi Arabia	24	2.71	.859
	Total	239	2.66	.987
Good quality of accommodation	UK	25	2.28	.542
	Netherlands	48	2.23	.660
	Germany	20	2.25	.639
	Norway	16	2.06	.574
	Denmark	15	2.27	.799
	Sweden	12	2.00	.603
	UAE	22	2.32	.995
	Egypt	20	1.80	.616
	Jordan	23	2.22	.902
	Qatar	11	2.18	.874
	Saudi Arabia	24	2.29	.751
	Total	236	2.19	.728
Good shopping facilities	UK	25	2.32	.690
	Netherlands	48	1.98	.785
	Germany	20	1.80	.768
	Norway	16	2.06	.574
	Denmark	15	1.87	.640
	Sweden	12	2.08	.669
	UAE	22	2.09	.811
	Egypt	20	2.00	.973
	Jordan	23	1.83	.717
	Qatar	12	2.00	.739
	Saudi Arabia	24	2.29	.955
	Total	237	2.03	.780
Rich cultural offer	UK	25	1.96	.735
	Netherlands	48	1.94	.909
	Germany	20	1.60	.940
	Norway	16	1.63	.719
	Denmark	15	1.87	.640
	Sweden	12	2.00	.739
	UAE	24	1.58	.584
	Egypt	20	1.95	.945
	Jordan	23	2.09	.793
	Qatar	12	1.83	.577
	Saudi Arabia	24	2.04	.624
	Total	239	1.87	.784
Brilliant nightlife	UK	25	2.36	.860

	Netherlands	48	2.19	.867
	Germany	20	1.85	.745
	Norway	16	2.56	.814
	Denmark	15	2.13	.743
	Sweden	12	2.08	.996
	UAE	24	1.92	.584
	Egypt	20	2.40	1.095
	Jordan	23	2.65	.832
	Qatar	12	2.50	.905
	Saudi Arabia	22	2.82	1.006
	Total	237	2.30	.893
Interesting historical sights	UK	25	1.84	.746
	Netherlands	48	1.58	.647
	Germany	20	1.45	.759
	Norway	16	1.69	.602
	Denmark	15	1.60	.632
	Sweden	12	1.67	.778
	UAE	24	1.67	.637
	Egypt	20	2.00	.649
	Jordan	23	2.00	.953
	Qatar	12	1.83	.718
	Saudi Arabia	24	2.00	.590
	Total	239	1.75	.713
Various parks/nature	UK	25	2.64	.952
	Netherlands	47	2.60	.925
	Germany	20	2.90	.968
	Norway	16	2.19	.655
	Denmark	15	2.47	.743
	Sweden	12	2.67	.888
	UAE	24	2.33	1.049
	Egypt	20	2.65	.875
	Jordan	23	1.87	.694
	Qatar	12	2.33	.778
	Saudi Arabia	24	2.25	.944
	Total	238	2.45	.912

Appendix 13

Detailed SPSS results for question 5

Descriptives

		N	Mean	Std. Deviation
Friendly people	Arab-Islamic	103	3.09	1.030
	Protestant European	136	2.61	.871
	Total	239	2.82	.970
Generally safe	Arab-Islamic	103	2.60	.821
	Protestant European	136	2.41	.735
	Total	239	2.49	.777
Clean	Arab-Islamic	103	1.99	.902
	Protestant European	136	2.60	.897
	Total	239	2.34	.947
Young	Arab-Islamic	101	2.51	.879
	Protestant European	135	2.55	.798
	Total	236	2.53	.832
Fun/Enjoyable	Arab-Islamic	101	2.29	.876
	Protestant European	136	2.17	.662
	Total	237	2.22	.761

ANOVA on Psychological Attributes

		Sum of Squares	df	F	Sig.
Friendly people	Between Groups	13.340	1	15.016	.000
	Within Groups	210.559	237		
	Total	223.900	238		
Generally safe	Between Groups	2.120	1	3.547	.061
	Within Groups	141.621	237		
	Total	143.741	238		
Clean	Between Groups	21.999	1	27.219	.000
	Within Groups	191.549	237		
	Total	213.548	238		
Young	Between Groups	.064	1	.092	.762
	Within Groups	162.665	234		
	Total	162.729	235		
Fun/Enjoyable	Between Groups	.807	1	1.397	.238
	Within Groups	135.784	235		
	Total	136.591	236		

Level of Agreement in Mean Values for each attribute by Nationality

		N	Mean	Std. Deviation
Friendly people	UK	25	2.80	1.041
	Netherlands	48	2.56	.848
	Germany	20	2.80	.894
	Norway	16	2.31	.479
	Denmark	15	2.47	.834
	Sweden	12	2.67	.985
	UAE	24	2.38	.970
	Egypt	20	3.50	.889
	Jordan	23	3.26	.915
	Qatar	12	3.00	1.044
	Saudi Arabia	24	3.33	1.007
	Total	239	2.82	.970
Generally safe	UK	25	2.56	.768
	Netherlands	48	2.54	.683
	Germany	20	2.70	.923
	Norway	16	2.00	.516
	Denmark	15	2.13	.516
	Sweden	12	2.00	.603
	UAE	24	2.71	.999
	Egypt	20	2.70	.865
	Jordan	23	2.39	.722
	Qatar	12	2.42	.793
	Saudi Arabia	24	2.71	.690
	Total	239	2.49	.777
Clean	UK	25	2.48	.714
	Netherlands	48	2.73	.869
	Germany	20	3.20	1.152
	Norway	16	2.19	.750
	Denmark	15	2.33	.724
	Sweden	12	2.25	.754
	UAE	24	2.21	1.021
	Egypt	20	2.00	1.170
	Jordan	23	2.04	.475
	Qatar	12	1.92	.793
	Saudi Arabia	24	1.75	.897
	Total	239	2.34	.947
Young	UK	25	2.76	.779
	Netherlands	48	2.56	.873
	Germany	20	2.25	.550
	Norway	15	2.80	.414
	Denmark	15	2.40	.737

	Sweden	12	2.42	1.165
	UAE	24	2.33	.761
	Egypt	20	2.55	.759
	Jordan	21	2.81	1.209
	Qatar	12	2.17	.577
	Saudi Arabia	24	2.58	.830
	Total	236	2.53	.832
Fun/Enjoyable	UK	25	2.28	.678
	Netherlands	48	2.10	.660
	Germany	20	2.15	.489
	Norway	16	2.38	.719
	Denmark	15	2.00	.535
	Sweden	12	2.17	.937
	UAE	24	2.04	.751
	Egypt	20	2.30	.865
	Jordan	22	2.32	.716
	Qatar	11	2.45	1.293
	Saudi Arabia	24	2.42	.929
	Total	237	2.22	.761

Appendix 14

Detailed SPSS results for question 6

Descriptives

		N	Mean	Std. Deviation
Vivid cityscape	Arab-Islamic	101	2.53	.986
	Protestant European	136	2.01	.765
	Total	237	2.23	.903
Green	Arab-Islamic	103	2.43	1.035
	Protestant European	136	2.95	.937
	Total	239	2.72	1.012
Multi-cultural	Arab-Islamic	101	2.35	.974
	Protestant European	136	2.04	.902
	Total	237	2.17	.943
Well-groomed	Arab-Islamic	99	2.47	.719
	Protestant European	134	2.63	.700
	Total	233	2.57	.711
Noble/Classy	Arab-Islamic	102	2.63	.843
	Protestant European	132	2.85	.869

	Total	234	2.75	.863
Beautiful	Arab-Islamic	102	2.27	.846
	Protestant European	136	2.44	.941
	Total	238	2.37	.903
Tolerant	Arab-Islamic	103	2.64	.850
	Protestant European	134	2.51	.829
	Total	237	2.57	.839
Modern	Arab-Islamic	103	1.75	.696
	Protestant European	135	2.15	.797
	Total	238	1.97	.779

ANOVA on Functional Holistic Factors

		Sum of Squares	df	F	Sig.
Vivid cityscape	Between Groups	16.115	1	21.502	.000
	Within Groups	176.121	235		
	Total	192.236	236		
Green	Between Groups	15.930	1	16.571	.000
	Within Groups	227.844	237		
	Total	243.774	238		
Multi-cultural	Between Groups	5.301	1	6.088	.014
	Within Groups	204.607	235		
	Total	209.907	236		
Well-groomed	Between Groups	1.450	1	2.893	.090
	Within Groups	115.769	231		
	Total	117.219	232		
Noble/Classy	Between Groups	2.811	1	3.818	.052
	Within Groups	170.813	232		
	Total	173.624	233		
Beautiful	Between Groups	1.619	1	1.992	.159
	Within Groups	191.843	236		
	Total	193.462	237		
Tolerant	Between Groups	1.035	1	1.472	.226
	Within Groups	165.201	235		
	Total	166.236	236		
Modern	Between Groups	9.375	1	16.453	.000
	Within Groups	134.474	236		
	Total	143.849	237		

Level of agreement in mean values by nationality

Descriptives

		N	Mean	Std. Deviation
Vivid cityscape	UK	25	1.88	.526
	Netherlands	48	2.19	.867
	Germany	20	1.70	.657
	Norway	16	1.81	.750
	Denmark	15	2.27	.704
	Sweden	12	2.00	.853
	UAE	23	2.39	.988
	Egypt	19	2.11	.937
	Jordan	23	2.87	1.058
	Qatar	12	2.75	1.138
	Saudi Arabia	24	2.58	.776
	Total	237	2.23	.903
Green	UK	25	2.80	1.041
	Netherlands	48	3.17	.859
	Germany	20	3.45	.887
	Norway	16	2.44	.814
	Denmark	15	2.53	.834
	Sweden	12	2.75	.866
	UAE	24	2.79	1.215
	Egypt	20	2.60	.940
	Jordan	23	2.26	.915
	Qatar	12	2.42	.996
	Saudi Arabia	24	2.08	.974
	Total	239	2.72	1.012
Multi-cultural	UK	25	2.44	1.083
	Netherlands	48	2.21	.874
	Germany	20	1.45	.605
	Norway	16	1.88	.885
	Denmark	15	2.00	.756
	Sweden	12	1.83	.718
	UAE	23	1.74	.541
	Egypt	19	2.68	1.204
	Jordan	23	2.70	1.185
	Qatar	12	2.17	.835
	Saudi Arabia	24	2.42	.654
	Total	237	2.17	.943
	UK	25	2.80	.764

	UK	25	2.80	.764
Well-groomed	Germany	20	2.40	.681
	Norway	16	2.69	.602
	Denmark	15	2.40	.737
	Sweden	11	2.27	.786
	UAE	22	2.27	.703
	Egypt	19	2.42	.961
	Jordan	22	2.77	.685
	Qatar	12	2.42	.669
	Saudi Arabia	24	2.46	.509
	Total	233	2.57	.711
Noble/Classy	UK	25	2.96	.790
	Netherlands	46	2.80	.833
	Germany	20	3.20	1.105
	Norway	15	2.93	.799
	Denmark	15	2.47	.743
	Sweden	11	2.55	.820
	UAE	23	2.52	.898
	Egypt	20	2.55	.759
	Jordan	23	2.61	.988
	Qatar	12	2.67	.778
	Saudi Arabia	24	2.79	.779
	Total	234	2.75	.863
Beautiful	UK	25	2.80	.866
	Netherlands	48	2.40	.984
	Germany	20	2.85	.988
	Norway	16	2.25	.856
	Denmark	15	1.93	.704
	Sweden	12	2.08	.793
	UAE	23	2.04	.638
	Egypt	20	2.30	.923
	Jordan	23	2.09	.793
	Qatar	12	2.42	.793
	Saudi Arabia	24	2.58	.974
	Total	238	2.37	.903
	UK	25	2.76	1.012
	Netherlands	47	2.49	.748
	Germany	20	2.45	.887
	Norway	16	2.25	.683
	Denmark	14	2.50	.519
	Sweden	12	2.50	1.087
	UAE	24	2.50	.933
	Egypt	20	2.95	.945
	Jordan	23	2.48	.947
	Qatar	12	2.50	.674

	Saudi Arabia	24	2.75	.608
	Total	237	2.57	.839
Modern	UK	25	2.08	.759
	Netherlands	47	2.30	.883
	Germany	20	2.25	.786
	Norway	16	2.38	.806
	Denmark	15	1.73	.458
	Sweden	12	1.75	.622
	UAE	24	1.96	.751
	Egypt	20	1.70	.571
	Jordan	23	1.65	.573
	Qatar	12	1.67	.778
	Saudi Arabia	24	1.71	.806
	Total	238	1.97	.779

Appendix 15

Detailed SPSS results for question 7

Descriptives

		N	Mean	Std. Deviation
Pleasant	Arab-Islamic	103	2.17	.648
	Protestant European	136	2.05	.588
	Total	239	2.10	.616
Lively/Dynamic	Arab-Islamic	102	2.22	.726
	Protestant European	136	1.98	.745
	Total	238	2.08	.745
Exciting	Arab-Islamic	103	2.19	.817
	Protestant European	136	2.15	.815
	Total	239	2.17	.815
Entertaining	Arab-Islamic	103	2.09	.688
	Protestant European	136	2.10	.676
	Total	239	2.09	.680
Attractive/Interesting	Arab-Islamic	103	2.11	.670
	Protestant European	135	1.87	.674
	Total	238	1.97	.681
Charming	Arab-Islamic	100	2.60	.985
	Protestant European	132	2.64	.876
	Total	232	2.62	.923

Trendy/Cool	Arab-Islamic	101	2.33	.873
	Protestant European	136	2.38	.942
	Total	237	2.35	.912
Creative/Innovative	Arab-Islamic	103	2.19	.864
	Protestant European	135	2.35	.822
	Total	238	2.28	.842
Good atmosphere for tourists	Arab-Islamic	103	2.30	.802
	Protestant European	135	2.20	.799
	Total	238	2.24	.800

ANOVA on Psychological Holistic Factors

		Sum of Squares	df	F	Sig.
Pleasant	Between Groups	.891	1	2.359	.126
	Within Groups	89.494	237		
	Total	90.385	238		
Lively/Dynamic	Between Groups	3.294	1	6.065	.015
	Within Groups	128.189	236		
	Total	131.483	237		
Exciting	Between Groups	.093	1	.139	.709
	Within Groups	157.874	237		
	Total	157.967	238		
Entertaining	Between Groups	.004	1	.009	.927
	Within Groups	109.971	237		
	Total	109.975	238		
Attractive/Interesting	Between Groups	3.164	1	7.000	.009
	Within Groups	106.685	236		
	Total	109.849	237		
Charming	Between Groups	.075	1	.088	.767
	Within Groups	196.545	230		
	Total	196.621	231		
Trendy/Cool	Between Groups	.135	1	.162	.688
	Within Groups	196.093	235		
	Total	196.228	236		
Creative/Innovative	Between Groups	1.385	1	1.960	.163
	Within Groups	166.754	236		
	Total	168.139	237		

Good atmosphere for tourists	Between Groups	.596	1	.929	.336
	Within Groups	151.270	236		
	Total	151.866	237		

Level of agreement in mean values by nationality

		N	Mean	Std. Deviation
Pleasant	UK	25	2.12	.600
	Netherlands	48	1.98	.565
	Germany	20	2.35	.671
	Norway	16	2.06	.443
	Denmark	15	2.00	.655
	Sweden	12	1.75	.452
	UAE	24	2.04	.550
	Egypt	20	2.50	1.051
	Jordan	23	2.13	.344
	Qatar	12	2.25	.452
	Saudi Arabia	24	2.04	.550
	Total	239	2.10	.616
Lively/Dynamic	UK	25	2.16	.746
	Netherlands	48	1.92	.647
	Germany	20	1.65	.745
	Norway	16	2.00	.894
	Denmark	15	2.13	.743
	Sweden	12	2.17	.835
	UAE	23	2.00	.522
	Egypt	20	2.25	.910
	Jordan	23	2.26	.619
	Qatar	12	2.50	.905
	Saudi Arabia	24	2.21	.721
	Total	238	2.08	.745
Exciting	UK	25	2.28	.542
	Netherlands	48	2.25	.887
	Germany	20	2.10	.852
	Norway	16	2.00	.816
	Denmark	15	2.00	.845
	Sweden	12	2.00	.953
	UAE	24	1.79	.833
	Egypt	20	2.50	.827
	Jordan	23	2.13	.626
	Qatar	12	2.42	.669
	Saudi Arabia	24	2.29	.908

	Total	239	2.17	.815
Entertaining	UK	25	2.12	.526
	Netherlands	48	2.10	.722
	Germany	20	2.05	.686
	Norway	16	2.13	.806
	Denmark	15	2.07	.594
	Sweden	12	2.08	.793
	UAE	24	1.79	.779
	Egypt	20	2.15	.933
	Jordan	23	2.22	.422
	Qatar	12	2.25	.452
	Saudi Arabia	24	2.13	.612
	Total	239	2.09	.680
Attractive/Interesting	UK	25	1.92	.572
	Netherlands	47	2.02	.766
	Germany	20	1.75	.639
	Norway	16	1.69	.602
	Denmark	15	1.73	.594
	Sweden	12	1.83	.718
	UAE	24	1.75	.794
	Egypt	20	2.30	.733
	Jordan	23	2.17	.576
	Qatar	12	2.25	.622
	Saudi Arabia	24	2.17	.482
	Total	238	1.97	.681
Charming	UK	24	2.71	.806
	Netherlands	48	2.81	.842
	Germany	20	2.70	.923
	Norway	14	2.29	.825
	Denmark	15	2.13	.990
	Sweden	11	2.73	.786
	UAE	23	1.96	1.022
	Egypt	20	2.60	1.046
	Jordan	23	2.91	.900
	Qatar	12	2.75	.965
	Saudi Arabia	22	2.86	.710
	Total	232	2.62	.923
Trendy/Cool	UK	25	2.48	.918
	Netherlands	48	2.44	.965
	Germany	20	2.55	.826
	Norway	16	2.25	.683
	Denmark	15	1.87	.834
	Sweden	12	2.42	1.379
	UAE	23	2.04	.825
	Egypt	20	2.35	.988

	Jordan	23	2.65	.714
	Qatar	12	2.42	.996
	Saudi Arabia	23	2.22	.850
	Total	237	2.35	.912
Creative/Innovative	UK	25	2.32	.627
	Netherlands	48	2.54	.898
	Germany	19	2.37	.955
	Norway	16	2.06	.574
	Denmark	15	2.27	.884
	Sweden	12	2.08	.793
	UAE	24	2.04	.806
	Egypt	20	2.00	.649
	Jordan	23	2.48	.665
	Qatar	12	2.08	.793
	Saudi Arabia	24	2.29	1.197
	Total	238	2.28	.842
Good atmosphere for tourists	UK	24	2.08	.830
	Netherlands	48	2.23	.778
	Germany	20	2.30	.865
	Norway	16	2.06	.929
	Denmark	15	2.00	.655
	Sweden	12	2.58	.669
	UAE	24	1.79	.658
	Egypt	20	2.45	.759
	Jordan	23	2.48	.665
	Qatar	12	2.17	.835
	Saudi Arabia	24	2.58	.881
	Total	238	2.24	.800

Appendix 16

Detailed SPPS results for question 8

How do you rate your overall image of Berlin as a tourist destination?

		Frequency	Percent	Valid Percent	Cumulative Percent
Valid	Very positive	35	14.6	14.7	14.7
	Positive	128	53.6	53.8	68.5

		57	23.8	23.9	92.4
	Neutral	57	23.8	23.9	92.4
	Negative	18	7.5	7.6	100.0
	Total	238	99.6	100.0	
Missing	System	1	.4		
Total		239	100.0		

Descriptives

How do you rate your overall image of Berlin as a tourist destination?

	N	Mean	Std. Deviation
	Lower Bound	Upper Bound	Lower Bound
Arab-Islamic	103	2.50	.752
Protestant European	135	2.04	.771
Total	238	2.24	.795

ANOVA

How do you rate your overall image of Berlin as a tourist destination?

	Sum of Squares	df	F	Sig.
Between Groups	12.385	1	21.259	.000
Within Groups	137.481	236		
Total	149.866	237		

Curriculum Vitae

Wassim El Kadhi

-MA (Arts) European Tourism Management-
-BA (Arts) International Tourism Management-

Date of Birth: 10/08/1982   **Nationality:** German / Tunisian

Marital Status: Single   **Language skills:** German, English, French, Arab

E-Mail: Welkadhi@gmail.com

Education

2007-2008: MA (Arts) European Tourism Management at Bournemouth University
→1st stage NHTV Breda (Holland)
→2nd stage Université de Savoie (France)
→3rd stage FH Heilbronn (Germany) (Erasmus)

2004-2007: BA (Arts) International Tourism Management at Bournemouth University
Dissertation: 'Do Southern English airline passengers consider airlines' environmental commitment / policy in their purchase decision making? And can airlines gain a competitive advantage by being environmentally responsible?'

1995-2002: Bertha-von-Suttner Gymnasium (~ High School) in Berlin
Qualification: Abitur (~ A-levels)

Employment

Since 12/08:   Junior Sales Manager, Eichbaum Brauereien AG, Mannheim (Germany)

12/05-06/06:   Security and Door Supervisor, Opium Security, Bournemouth

05/06-03/07:   Agent at United World School of English, Bournemouth

11/05-02/06:   Work placement at Brittany Ferries, Poole Harbour (UK)

03/05-10/05:   Cashier, Ladbrokes Racing Ltd., Bournemouth

03/04-06/04:   Griller and Waiter, Nando's Restaurant, Bournemouth (UK)

10/02-06/03:   Pioneer and Trained driver, German Army, Havelberg (Germany)

04/02-07/02:   Telephone marketing, 'Weinhaus Bacchus', Berlin

---

Interests

Economy, Stock Exchange, Airline Industry, Cultures, Global Warming, Marine Creatures, Sports, Cars